FRONTIER
GRIT

The author's great-aunt Alice Robbins (left), born in 1893, pheasant hunting with a friend in Oregon.

FRONTIER GRIT

GRIT

The Unlikely True Stories
of Daring Pioneer Women

MARIANNE MONSON

SHADOW
MOUNTAIN

To my pioneer ancestors both literal and metaphorical,
and to Aria, pioneer girl rising

Photo credits:

page ii: Courtesy of Alice Allred, used by permission.

page 1: Nellie Cashman, courtesty of Arizona Historical Society, Tucson, AHS #1847.

page 19: Clara Brown, photo in public domain.

page 35: Abigail Scott Duniway voting, courtesy of The Oregonian, *used by permission.*

page 53: María Amparo Ruiz de Burton, photo in public domain.

page 69: While this is not a hotel Luzena operated, it is representative of the hotels at that time. Metropolitan Hotel, courtesy of Library of Congress.

page 83: Mother Jones, © Everett Historical/shutterstock.com.

page 97: Zitkala-Sa, photo in public domain.

page 113: Mary Hallock Foote, courtesy of Idaho State Historical Society, image #63-238.12.

page 114: A Pretty Girl in the West, by Mary Hallock Foote, courtesy of Library of Congress.

page 129: Martha Hughes Cannon, used by permission, Utah State Historical Society, USHS 11877.

page 147: Donaldina Cameron and Chinese girl, used by permission, courtesy of Cameron House.

page 167: There is no known photo of Charley Parkhurst. Photo of stagecoach © Everett Historical/shutterstock.com.

page 179: There is no known photo of Makaopiopio. Map © Steven Wynn/istock.

Library of Congress Cataloging-in-Publication Data

Names: Monson, Marianne, 1975–   author.

Title: Frontier grit : the unlikely true stories of daring pioneer women / Marianne Monson.

Description: Salt Lake City, Utah : Shadow Mountain, [2016] | ©2016 | Includes bibliographical references.

Identifiers: LCCN 2016011148 (print) | LCCN 2016012793 (ebook) | ISBN 9781629722276 (hardbound : alk. paper) | ISBN 9781629734682 (ebook)

Subjects: LCSH: Women pioneers—United States—Biography. | United States—History—1865–1921—Biography. | LCGFT: Biographies.

Classification: LCC E663 .M73 2016 (print) | LCC E663 (ebook) | DDC 920.72—dc23

LC record available at http://lccn.loc.gov/2016011148

Printed in the United States of America

Publishers Printing, Salt Lake City, UT

10   9   8   7   6   5   4   3   2   1

CONTENTS

"When I stop at one of the graveyards in my own county . . .
I have always the hope that something went into the ground
with those pioneers that will one day come out again."

—Willa Cather

INTRODUCTION

What constitutes a frontier? Is it simply an imaginary boundary between geographical spaces? Or is it a constantly moving line between supposed "civilization" and the "unknown" beyond? As I set out to write on the topic of female pioneers, all attempts inevitably drew me back to this elusive term. The boundaries of the United States shifted steadily throughout the nineteenth century, creating a multitude of frontiers by every definition.

To me, a frontier is simply a place where your people have not gone before—it is the place on the map where the collective thinking of your society draws a large and compelling question mark. Of course, this doesn't have to be a geographical boundary—it might be an unexplored theological issue, an uncomfortable topic of conversation, an unfolding intellectual sphere, a newly invented technology, or an insight irreconcilable with current social norms.

And although no one you personally know has been to such a space, that doesn't mean it has never been inhabited by another group of people who have a prior claim to it. But because no one *you* know has been there, the frontier is a place where rules are still being worked out and negotiated—it is space available to anyone, not only the powerful players of the past.

The freedom of such a space is as exhilarating as it is disconcerting, and, in a true frontier, the traditional safeguards and protections are as glaringly absent as the stifling rules. People can and will get hurt. That is why rules were made in the first place, at least hypothetically.

I was raised on stories of strong pioneer women who traversed frontier spaces. Within my own family history, I have women who left lives of luxury in England, positions of leadership among the Maori in New Zealand, and others who were drawn by their poverty from the hamlets of Wales. Some of my ancestors set up house in an abandoned chicken coop. I was raised on these stories. The blood of these women runs through my veins, and I grew up seeing my life as a continuation of their own.

And in fact, all of our lives are such a continuation. The frontier as we've defined it could as easily apply to modern technology, with its resulting onslaught of related inventions, as it does to the American West. We live today in a world of upheaval, a world changing at a frantic pace, where many boundaries of the past have been flung away, and we are once again deciding: What are the rules? And who gets to say? Now, more than ever, we need to know the stories of the women whose blood runs through our veins, literally or metaphorically.

While working on this project, I came across a box of books discarded by my university's library. Never one to pass up free books, I sorted through the stack and found an old, leather-bound volume entitled *Pioneers of California*. Thinking it might be useful, I thumbed through the pages. Chapter after chapter of the book profiled ministers, governors, politicians, settlers, and gold rushers to the West. Without a single exception, they were white. Without a single exception, they were all male.

The book served as a reminder that we are not many generations removed from a time when it was perfectly acceptable to tell the story of California through the eyes of white males alone. But history is made up of so much more than established war heroes and political figures. It is made up of people—their stories, failures, and triumphs. As the historian Howard Zinn has observed, "If history is to be creative, to anticipate new possibilities without denying the past, it should, I believe, emphasize new possibilities by disclosing those hidden episodes of the past when, even if in brief flashes, people showed their ability to resist, to join together, occasionally to win. I am supposing, or perhaps only hoping, that our future may be found in the past's fugitive moments of compassion rather than in its solid centuries of warfare."[1]

Thousands of women—black, white, Native American, Mexican, Chinese, Polynesian, and other racial variations—experienced the physical frontier space of the American West. As the "pioneers of California" can be broadened to include women, so can the term be redefined beyond the special province of American expansionism. The women in this book come from a variety of backgrounds and traveled in a number of different directions—these stories represent a mere handful of the women who survived and even thrived on a multitude of gritty, tumultuous frontiers. Some were crushed by the challenge, their voices silenced and discarded in the passing of time. But some of them triumphed; some of their stories remain. In spite of all odds stacked against them, their voices persist, speaking through a journal kept in a leaky wagon or through a life so remarkable the world was forced to take note.

Fragments of their stained, complicated, gloriously real lives have been passed on to us, giving us tales to fuel our own efforts to build on these "fugitive moments of compassion," and create lives that become stories worth telling. The further I got into this project, the more I marveled at the contemporary relevance of these women. So many of the questions that still haunt and inspire us, both as individuals and as a nation, can be traced to the historical events surrounding their lives. You will be astonished at how familiar their struggles appear, and I can promise you will find yourself in these pages.

In this book I have attempted to avoid political language—retaining interpretation to the end of each chapter, and maintaining objectivity as much as possible, while acknowledging that no history is ever truly objective. There are far too many divisions in U.S. society today, and my hope is that by focusing on principles, discussion, and compassion, we may begin to bridge some of those gaps and divides. In places where you find yourself disagreeing with my interpretation, please take what you find helpful and disregard the rest.

Pioneering of every variety, in every generation, requires a stubbornness of thought, a willingness to disregard public opinion, and a grit to endure. These stories are fit inspiration for modern-day efforts to venture into new and unknown paths, climb ragged, rocky mountains, and harness a vision of how we might rebuild this tumultuous world into something better, truer, and stronger for generations yet to come. May you find impetus here to forge your own frontier.

NOTE

1. Howard Zinn, *A People's History of the United States* (New York: Harper Perennial, 2005), 11.

CHAPTER 1

NELLIE CASHMAN
GOLD RUSH "BOOMER"

Born: 1845, County Cork, Ireland
Died: January 4, 1925, Victoria, Vancouver Island, Canada

"Why don't you go West, young woman?
The West needs people like you."[1]

The life of Nellie Cashman is made from the stuff of frontier yarns spun by the light of a glowing fire. With each telling, the stories grow more fantastic, supernatural, and unbelievable, until trying to separate the truth from the myths of her life is a lot like the work Nellie loved best—swirling a pan filled with silt and river water—turning it, turning it, turning it—watching for the briefest sparks of gold. Drawn by hopes of the mother lode, Nellie travelled the whole of the West, settling in outposts from Mexico in the south to the Yukon in the north. More than just the hope of striking it rich drove Nellie forward, however; it was pioneering she loved, in all its dirty, rough-tumbled glory. She reveled in the harshest and most demanding environments, where she could pit her indomitable will against nature's forces, where people relied on each other for survival without any of the fancy trappings of society. When the outposts of California and Arizona became too civilized for Nellie, she moved on to places that remain frontiers to this day. In her eighties, she mushed a dog sled 750 miles in seventeen days across the frozen tundra of northern Alaska. This remarkable woman never tired of finding new ways to test her own endurance and will to survive.

To understand how Nellie Cashman developed the character-istics manifest in the American West, we return to Ireland in the 1840s, where absentee British landlords owned eighty percent of the land. Ruling from afar, this gentry class forced the Irish working poor to raise crops on behalf of corrupt overseers. While Ireland produced a wide variety of foods, the poor existed on one crop as the basis of their diet—the potato. When the potato crop failed multiple years in a row due to blight, starvation set in. In an appalling irony, Ireland continued to export grains and other foods throughout the famine. For this reason, many historians today consider the period known in Ireland as the Great Hunger to be genocide rather than famine. It is estimated that more than one million people died and another one million emigrated—a loss that amounted to more than twenty-five percent of the country within a few short years.

Nellie later referred to the famine as Ireland's "unequal contest between want and oppression."[2] Though it is unclear precisely when in 1845 Nellie was born and at what age she left Ireland behind, it is undeniable that her native land left a deep and lasting impres-sion. From her early years, she emerged with a deep devotion to her Catholic religion, an immense appreciation for the freedom of the United States, a healthy disregard for the wealthy classes, and an awareness of what it means to suffer. She also established a pattern of leaving one place behind in search of a new beginning.

From limited records, it appears that Nellie's father may have been one of the million Irish who died in the famine; others say he lived to take his family to Boston. With or without her husband, Nellie's mother and her daughters sailed for America in a "coffin ship," whose notoriously tight quarters and inadequate food ran rampant with disease. The women landed in Boston, where the working class resented the arrival of desperate Irishmen willing to work for a pittance. "No Irish Need Apply" signs hung in many shop windows, and the people of Boston—by and large—considered the Irish to be "a servant race."[3] Despite this, the women managed to find work and stayed in Boston for roughly fifteen years. Nellie found employment as a bellhop in a hotel for part of that time, where she once attended to General Ulysses S. Grant. The story goes that when she told the general she wanted to "do things" with her life, he replied, "Why don't you go West, young woman? The West needs people like you."[4]

She certainly did. Traveling with her mother, Frances, and sister Fannie, Nellie made her way to San Francisco. Some accounts say they went by ship via Panama, but the more likely scenario is that the women traveled by train on a special immigrant fare of forty dollars.[5] Nellie arrived in San Francisco and fell in love with the rugged freedom of the West, where anything was possible and even an Irish girl could strike it rich. Irish made up a third of the population of San Francisco, and the strong anti-Irish Catholic sentiment primarily remained behind in the "civilized" world of the East.

Shortly after the women arrived, Nellie's sister Fannie became engaged to another Irish immigrant. In the prospering town of San Francisco, Nellie surely had plenty of marriage opportunities, but she stayed single, saying she "preferred to being pals with men to being cook for one man."[6] While Fannie settled into married life, Nellie decided to explore, yearning for gold, opportunity, and adventure. Though details from these years are scarce and accounts contradictory, it appears tales of rich-paying silver mines in Nevada drew Nellie and her mother first to Virginia City, then on to rough-and-tumble Pioche, Nevada, notorious for brawls and gunfights. A lack of law enforcement took its toll on the town—in fact, seventy-two graves dotted Boot Hill before a single soul in Pioche died of natural causes. The settlement contained gold rushers, Mexicans, and Indians, but precious few women. Pioche had already blown up and burned once before the women got there and boasted no fewer than seventy-two saloons and thirty-two brothels.[7]

A location as remote and rough as this one would hardly seem like a natural choice for two single women, but Nellie fell in love with both the miners and the mining way of life. One gold rusher said the biggest attractions of the lifestyle were "independence and absolute equality in the world of chance,"[8] a description that couldn't stand in greater contrast to the injustice Nellie had witnessed in Ireland. In Pioche, fortunes arose one day and burned to the ground the next. Intense freedom existed alongside intense suffering. Deeply energized by the appeal of "life at full tide,"[9] Nellie set two goals for herself: the first was to make a great deal of money; the second was to help anyone in need along the way.

In a pattern she would repeat many times, Nellie prospected for silver and opened a boardinghouse to supply a steady source of income. She never stayed long in one place. As soon as mining declined in one area, new reports of gold discoveries trickled in and Nellie's itch for excitement drew her off, looking for new horizons to explore. Often termed "boomers," gold rushers of this variety stayed in town for the initial mining boom and then made their way to the next.

In 1873, the Pioche mines began to decline. Now in her twenties, Nellie settled her mother in San Jose and convinced an all-male party of miners to let Nellie join their prospecting expedition to British Columbia's Northern Interior. A few hours south of the Yukon border, the Cassiar district had rarely been explored by anyone outside of native communities, and Nellie claimed to be the first white woman to see its dizzying glories, where the searing heights of the Rocky Mountains descend to frozen blue glaciers. Mountain goats inhabit the rocky peaks, and dense evergreen forests teem with grizzly bear and moose. The thundering Stikine River is a river so wild that to navigate it is comparable to scaling the heights of Everest. Nearby, on the edge of Dease Lake, Nellie operated a boardinghouse and saloon and prospected surrounding streams and creeks.

When the weather turned chill, Nellie left her mining comrades behind, heading south to Victoria to wait for the arrival of spring. Shortly after her arrival, however, word came that early winter storms had trapped her friends in Cassiar without supplies. Three groups led by officers attempted to rescue the stranded miners, but unusually harsh conditions drove them back. Though she had never faced a winter in the far North, Nellie decided their recovery was in her hands alone, and she hired six men to assist the effort. Convinced she was heading to her death, many of her contemporaries tried to dissuade her. *The Victoria Daily Colonist* reported, "Her extraordinary freak of attempting to reach the diggings in midwinter and in the face of dangers and obstacles . . . is attributed by her friends as insanity."[10]

For seventy-seven days, Nellie's group traveled by snowshoe, pulling sleds packed tight with hundreds of pounds of potatoes, lime juice,[11] and other supplies. At times the trail entirely disappeared in a snowy abyss. When dogs could no longer pull through the deep drifts, Nellie strapped a sled to her own back and hauled it across the white expanse. Believing the party would never succeed, the commander at the nearest fort sent a rescue party to reclaim any survivors. When the troops showed up to "rescue" Nellie, they found her camped out on the frozen Stikine River, cooking supper over a campfire and whistling a merry tune. She invited the rescue party to take tea with her, and they later described her as "happy, contented, and comfortable."[12] Ever persuasive, Nellie managed to convince the group to return without her, contradicting their commander's orders. And so her rescue operation continued on its way, in spite of a few mishaps. For instance, one night an avalanche swept Nellie's tent a quarter mile downhill. Unfazed, she dug herself out and continued the mission.

By the time Nellie reached her former mining friends in Cassiar, they were extremely glad to see her. Several of the men had already succumbed to death from scurvy, and the survivors suffered from "bleeding sores and blackened limbs."[13] Nellie nursed the men with lifesaving lime juice and potatoes and proudly reported that no one else died after she arrived. This mission of mercy exalted Nellie from frontier woman to angel of mercy; many miners she rescued that day attributed miraculous powers to their hero, and the event prompted the bestowal upon her of the nickname "Angel of Cassiar."[14] Years later, one of the survivors on his death bed said, "If Nellie Cashman were only here, I'd get well."[15]

Beyond her miraculous survival, during the course of the rescue mission Nellie fell in love with the Cassiar wilderness. She remained two years more in the area, prospecting and running businesses to raise money for the construction of a Catholic hospital in Victoria. The poet and miner Robert Service, who also spent time in Cassiar, described the enchantment of this land in the following words: "The snows that are older than history, the woods where the weird shadows slant; the stillness, the moonlight, the mystery, I've bade 'em goodbye—but I can't." The landscape similarly enchanted Nellie, lingering in her memory for decades.

But if she returned from British Columbia ready for a change in weather, she certainly found it. After visiting family in San Francisco, Nellie wandered from Virginia City to Pioche, then on to Tucson, Arizona, where she briefly set up shop. In 1879, when silver mines began paying out at a new little mining outpost called Tombstone, she packed her bags and set off. The town of Tombstone resembled the early days of Pioche—a rough-and-tumble place filled with brothels, bars, and miners hungry for gold. A newcomer is said to have exclaimed, "All Tombstone needs to become the garden spot of the world is good people and water." A veteran prospector chuckled and responded, "Well stranger . . . I reckon that's all *hell* needs."[16] Nellie opened a variety of businesses, including the Nevada Boot and Shoe Store and the Arcade Restaurant and Chop House. She later focused on an upscale restaurant and hotel named Russ House, where patrons could choose from dishes such as lamb in caper sauce, beef á l'Espagnol, calf head in tortue, and chicken fricasee á la crème.

Both the famous and infamous found their way to Nellie's table. If they couldn't afford to pay, Nellie fed the hungry and the luckless for free. Legend has it that on one occasion a patron had a bit too much to drink and made a disparaging comment about the food served at Russ House. Doc Holliday, seated nearby, drew his revolver and pointed it at the patron. "What did you say about Miss Nellie's food, mister?" the mustachioed lawman inquired. "Food's delicious," the man amended. "Good as I've ever tasted." Doc Holliday returned his gun to his holster. "Yep, that's what I thought you said."[17]

From many reports, if Nellie wasn't running her businesses or buying mining claims, she was fundraising for one of many charitable causes. She grubstaked[18] miners down on their luck and raised five hundred dollars to help a miner who broke both legs in a mining accident. When an epidemic spread through town, Nellie turned Russ House into a makeshift hospital and helped nurse the sick herself. She fundraised for community efforts that led to Tombstone's first school and hospital, and when a local priest asked for help raising money to build a Catholic church, she staged the city's first theatrical production, a musical comedy entitled *The Irish Diamond*. Unlike other middle class women, Nellie accepted donations for her project from anyone who wanted to give—willingly working alongside both prostitutes and patrons. "Any man I ever met, if he needed my help, got it," Nellie said years later. "After all, we pass this way only once, and it's up to us to help our fellows when they need our help."[19]

Judging by Nellie's Tombstone years, she was making plenty of progress toward her twin goals of getting rich and helping others. All who knew her predicted her life would continue on as a series of breathtaking adventures. But life is seldom predictable—even for Nellie. In 1880, an unexpected telegram from Fannie turned Nellie's intentionally disordered world upside down.

While Nellie traipsed around the coast searching for ore, sister Fannie stayed in San Francisco with her husband, eventually giving birth to five children. Change in the form of tuberculosis, one of the most deadly nineteenth-century diseases, visited their home. After a battle of some months, Fannie's husband passed away, leaving her with five children to raise. When Nellie received the news, she immediately closed Russ House and joined her sister in San Francisco.

Realizing that it would be much easier to support the brood in Tombstone, however, the women returned to the mining town, where they reopened the boardinghouse and restaurant, though eventually Nellie sold Russ House and focused on running the American Hotel with her sister.

The children loved both their Aunt Nellie and the excitement of the frontier town, though sometimes things got a little rough. In 1882, fire burned much of Tombstone, in spite of the efforts of the bucket brigade. The fire damaged Nellie's hotel, but she had insured it generously, so it was soon rebuilt. Danger of a human-made variety also stalked the streets, and Mike Cunningham, the oldest of the children, later recalled the trauma of seeing the injured and the dead lying in the streets of Tombstone after the shootout at the O.K. Corral.

Nearby Bisbee also saw action of this kind, and on one occasion, when a string of innocent passersby died, the sheriff arrested and jailed the guilty parties. Nellie did not doubt their guilt, but her compassionate heart couldn't stand to see anyone suffer. She visited the prisoners, preaching religion out of concern for their immortal souls (her only known proselyting effort)—which seemed to be successful as she arranged the baptisms of several people.

City leaders decided to make a little profit from the hangings, and officials built a public execution site, permitting patrons to witness the scene for a price. The word on the street was that, due to their many enemies, the bodies of the guilty would not rest in the ground for long. The situation horrified Nellie, and she promised the prisoners she would do her part to see them safely in the ground after they received their just desserts. Armed with hatchets at two in the morning, a handful of hours before the hanging, Nellie led a silent mob to destroy the execution grandstands.[20] By morning the stage had been rendered into kindling wood. After the prisoners were executed in a less public manner, Nellie spent several nights in the graveyard with her shotgun, guarding the graves from desecration.

Wanderlust still visited Nellie, and in spite of her newly acquired family, she found time to lead an expedition to the Baja peninsula in 1883. Several variations of this story circulate—one version involves a Mexican who collapsed in the street. Nellie helped him inside, where he revealed nuggets of gold and said, "Mulege . . . go to Mulege" with his dying breath. The expedition through the Baja turned up very little gold and even less water, however. Nearly perishing from thirst, Nellie left the company and miraculously returned a day later with water to relieve the suffering. In some renditions of the tale, Nellie finds a mission home located near rich veins of gold, but promises the father that she won't reveal the location to hordes of gold seekers intent on overrunning the site. Nellie's biographers point out these stories are most certainly apocryphal, but their promulgation added to her fame. The only clearly established facts include the party's campaign to the Baja, where they failed to find gold, did not fare well in the extreme heat, and ended up in a Mexican jail cell, accused of commandeering a boat away from its drunk captain. Once they were released, the party returned to Tombstone with less gold in their pockets, but several new tales to tell.

In 1884, Fannie succumbed to the same disease that had taken her husband's life, and Nellie inherited five children, ages three to eleven. For three years, Nellie played the part of full-time mother to her nieces and nephews. As an adult, her nephew Tom recalled frequent baseball games in the vacant lot near the American Hotel. When squabbles over scores and losses grew loud enough for Nellie to hear, she hurried over and delivered a lecture on "self-control and sportsmanship," handing out slices of pie "to seal the truce."[21] Soon the clever boys staged fake altercations, figuring the lecture was worth enduring for the sake of the pie.

On another occasion, Mike and a friend decided to do some "prospecting" of their own. They packed up burros and rode fourteen miles into the Dragoon Mountains, an area made famous both for its silver deposits and roving bands of Apache Indians angered by mining activity on their land. The boys took shelter in an old cabin, but their courage faded along with the daylight. As Apache signal fires dotted the landscape, they huddled in one corner of the cabin, afraid for their lives. Fortunately, a prospector had recognized the boys on their way out of town and reported the escapade to Nellie. In the dark, she tracked them down to the cabin with the burros tied up outside. Through the open door she called, "Hello the house!" Flooded with relief, the two miscreants gratefully followed her back to Tombstone.[22]

The collapse of the mining industry in Tombstone in 1886 caused Nellie to close the doors of her hotel forever. Children in tow, she tried her luck in several spots in Montana and Wyoming but quickly realized this was no way to raise children. For one thing, the educational opportunities in mining towns were sketchy at best; for another, mining involved constant relocating. Concerned for their best interests, Nellie took the kids to San Francisco and settled them into a Catholic boarding school. Though this seems a hard solution by today's standards, Nellie maintained a good relationship with the children throughout their lives, writing often, maintaining financial support, and visiting them between mining expeditions.

Unencumbered once more, Nellie bounced around the West, following one mining boom after another. In 1897, the discovery of gold in the Klondike beckoned Nellie back to the white and frozen land she loved. She would spend the last two and a half decades of her life in Alaska, with periodic returns to visit family and friends. Just getting to Dawson proved the first adventure.

Nellie landed at Skagway, then drove a loaded dogsled 600 miles, wearing a fur hat, rubber boots, and men's trousers. Her intended route necessitated climbing the infamous Chilkoot Pass—twenty-six grueling miles so steep that horses and dogs cannot make the climb. Miners ascended on 1,500 stairs cut from ice, holding on to picks and guide ropes, with supplies and a sled strapped to their backs. The final four miles are practically vertical. As many as half of those who attempted the pass did not make it; they either fell to their death, turned back, or perished by avalanche. Nellie, with her sweet-talking brogue, somehow convinced the North-West Mounted Police that she could survive on less than the required supplies (one ton), and she conquered that pass. She camped that winter on Lake Laberge, and when the ice broke up on the Yukon River, she rode the rapids on a hand-built raft into town.

Once in Dawson, Nellie opened a restaurant and grocery store, and started staking out her claims. The mining was some of the most productive in her whole career, and she drew 100,000 dollars from the claim, much of which she gave to charity. Nellie said of Dawson, "That was a great place to meet interesting people."[23] Indeed, the Klondike Gold Rush drew all sorts, and Nellie enjoyed the company of writers Jack London, Joaquin Miller, and Captain Jack Crawford during her time there. Once again Nellie became the darling of the settlement, and legend has it that when fire threatened the town, Nellie asked for a bowl of holy water. According to several eyewitnesses, the moment she threw the water into the fire, the wind instantly changed direction, saving much of the city,[24] an incident that earned her the nickname "Doll of Dawson." Though Nellie loved the remoteness of Alaska, she would occasionally return to California to visit the children and be interviewed by the press. On one visit to California at the age of sixty-seven, Nellie was asked by a reporter if she planned to retire soon. She responded in the negative. "I'm mighty apt to make a million or two before I leave this romantic business of mining."[25]

Apparently even Dawson proved too sedate for Nellie. She moved on to Fairbanks, then continued to Nolan Creek at Coldfoot, sixty miles north of the Arctic Circle, an area inhabited by Koyukan Indians and a scant handful of the hardiest prospectors. Here she started the Midnight Sun Mining Company to fund her shaft mining enterprise. Increasingly reclusive, Nellie said, "It takes real folks to live by themselves in the lands of the north. . . . It takes the solitude of frozen nights with the howl of dogs for company, the glistening fairness of days when nature reaches out and loves you . . . to bring out the soul of folks. Banging trolley cars, honking horns, clubs for catty women, and false standards of living won't do it."[26]

In 1924, now in her seventies, Nellie took her last trip to the outside world. To get there, she drove a dogsled team 750 miles in seventeen days. Newspapers declared her the "champion musher of the world" for the accomplishment.[27] Her nephew Mike, now grown with a family of his own, begged her to stay in California, but she laughed and said, "I'm a long way from the cushion rocker stage"[28] and then shocked her family by returning to Alaska by airplane. For a few more years, Nellie continued her mining operations, but she finally ran out of adventures when she checked herself into the hospital in Victoria she had helped build forty years earlier. Eventually, this hardened wanderer succumbed to complications from pneumonia at the age of eighty.

☙❧

Nellie's life leaves me a bit breathless. Life was, to her, an endless thrill with a steady supply of new things to see, do, and try. She credited her youthful appearance with this lifestyle, and I wonder if perhaps she isn't right. In the words of Thoreau, "Life pines because it breathes its own breath over again."[29] Maybe Nellie stayed young because she constantly woke up to new possibilities. If you contrast her life with the one she might have spent in Boston, the disparity is phenomenal. I admire that in a world that viewed her as a poor Irish Catholic, she refused to accept society's estimation but dared to believe in another view of her gifts and abilities. She lived the mantra: "Go where you are celebrated, not merely tolerated."[30] Nellie crossed a continent in search of "her people," and she certainly found them. In the process, she also found a good deal of adrenaline and respect.

Her heart was as big as her thirst for gold, and this attribute tempered the gold fever that consumed many a miner. Nellie never forgot the reality of suffering, even when that suffering was not her own. To me, her legacy is one that says: push on until you find your place in this world, the place that fills you with fire and devotion. You're never too old to go looking for it, even if you have to search the whole world over. In the words of her obituary, "The 'old sourdough' has passed on, leaving many records behind—pioneer of Arizona, the first woman prospector in Alaska, the world's champion musher—but better by far than all of these is the fact that she lived—lived and enjoyed adventures that it is not given most the courage to taste."[31] In honor of Nellie, let us find our courage to do the same.

FURTHER READING

Don Chaput, *Nellie Cashman and the North American Mining Frontier* (Tucson, AZ: Westernlore Press, 2010).

Suzann Ledbetter, *Nellie Cashman: Prospector and Trailblazer* (El Paso: Texas Western Press, 1993).

Suzann Ledbetter, *Shady Ladies: Nineteen Surprising and Rebellious American Women* (New York: Tom Doherty Assoc., 2006).

Claire Rudolf Murphy and Jane G. Haigh, *Gold Rush Women* (Portland, OR: Alaska Northwest Books, 1997).

Sally Zanjani, *A Mine of Her Own: Women Prospectors in the American West, 1850–1950* (Lincoln: University of Nebraska Press, 1997).

NOTES

1. Suzann Ledbetter, *Nellie Cashman: Prospector and Trailblazer* (El Paso: Texas Western Press, 1993), 2.

2. Ibid.

3. University of Virginia. http://xroads.virginia.edu/~ug03/omara-alwala/irishkennedys.html.

4. Ledbetter, *Nellie Cashman*, 2.

5. Frances Laurence, *Maverick Women: 19th Century Women Who Kicked Over the Traces* (N.p.: Manifest Publications, 1998).

6. Ledbetter, *Nellie Cashman*, 3.

7. Sally Zanjani, *A Mine of Her Own: Women Prospectors in the American West, 1850–1950* (Lincoln: University of Nebraska Press, 1997), 30.

8. Ibid., 31.

9. Ibid.

10. Ledbetter, *Nellie Cashman*, 7.

11. Potatoes and lime juice were known remedies for scurvy.

12. Zanjani, *Mine of Her Own*, 34.

13. Ibid., 35.

14. Ibid., 26.

15. Ledbetter, *Nellie Cashman*, 7.

16. Ibid., 14.

17. Ibid., 19.

18. "Grubstaking" is a mining term for lending a prospector money to continue his or her efforts, expecting to see a return on the profits.

19. Suzann Ledbetter, *Shady Ladies: Nineteen Surprising and Rebellious American Women* (New York: Tom Doherty Assoc., 2006), 105.

20. Some sources indicate that Nellie did not, in fact, lead the efforts to destroy the grandstand, though she supported the endeavor. Ron Fischer, in an interview with Mike Cunningham's stepdaughter, confirmed that Mike certainly believed that Nellie led the attack (see Ron W. Fischer, *Nellie Cashman: Frontier Angel* [Honolulu, HI: Talei Publishers, 2000]).

21. Ledbetter, *Shady Ladies*, 31.

22. Zanjani, *Mine of Her Own*, 46.

23. Ledbetter, *Nellie Cashman*, 48.

24. Zanjani, *Mine of Her Own*, 54.

25. Ibid., 57.

26. Ledbetter, *Nellie Cashman*, 51.

27. Karen Surina Mulford, *Trailblazers: Twenty Amazing Western Women* (Flagstaff, AZ: Northland Publishing, 2001), 46.

28. Ledbetter, *Nellie Cashman*, 48.

29. Henry David Thoreau, *Walden* (New York: T.Y. Crowell & Company, 1899), 219.

30. Paul F. Davis, quoted at https://www.goodreads.com/quotes/126432-if-you-don-t-feel-it-flee-from-it-go-where.

31. Ledbetter, *Shady Ladies*, 107.

CHAPTER 2

AUNT CLARA BROWN
A WOMAN IN A THOUSAND

Born: Circa 1800, Virginia
Died: October 1885, Denver, Colorado

"Rising from the humble position of a slave to the angelic type of a noble woman, [she] won our sympathy and commanded our respect."[1]

The story of Clara Brown reads like the most compelling of fiction—filled with drama, heartache, adventure, and a plucky heroine who refuses to give up under any conditions. It is only a matter of time before Hollywood gets its hands on this tale of heartbreak and loss, of triumph over gut-wrenching odds. Clara's debut upon the world stage occurred in one of the darkest chapters in American history—somewhere around the year 1800 in a small slave cabin deep in the heart of Virginia.

During Clara's life, the Supreme Court ruled on the controversial case of *Dred Scott v. Sandford*. Hoping to settle the racial debate forever, Chief Justice Taney declared that blacks were "beings of an inferior order, and altogether unfit to associate with the white race, either in social or political relations."[2]

This was the world of Clara's birth, a world that did not record the exact date of the occasion. Also, as was typical for babies born into slavery, Clara was given no last name. When she was only three, her father and older brother were auctioned to the highest bidder; Clara would never see them again.[3] A farmer named Ambrose Smith purchased both Clara and her mother. Six years later, the Smith family decided to "go west," to the wilds of Kentucky. The group traveled through the Appalachian Mountains on a road originally cut by Daniel Boone.[4] It was young Clara's first taste of pioneering, and it left a deep impression.

The Smith family and their slaves cleared and cultivated the new land allotment in order to build a plantation home with a row of slave cabins away from the main house. Clara helped her mother with the cooking, laundering, and cow milking, all relentless tasks on a busy frontier farm.[5] Young Clara learned to dry herbs, make blueberry preserves, pack meat in barrels of rock salt, kill chickens, and prepare a tasty stew: these proved to be valuable skills she would use for the rest of her life.

On Sundays, the Smiths allowed Clara and her mother to travel with them to the Methodist chapel, a rather atypical practice among slave owners. Traveling preachers held popular revival meetings, drawing crowds from all over Kentucky. During one service, Clara said the spirit of God spoke to her powerfully, promising to guide and protect her always. From that moment on, Clara believed that God would see her through all difficulties she might be called upon to face. In later years, she recalled, "When I was a girl, I relied on His mercy, and He fetched me through."[6]

Clara was eighteen years old when the Smith family purchased a new slave—a strong and handsome carpenter named Richard. Smitten with Clara, he asked for her hand in marriage. Clara agreed, and Master Smith gave his consent along with an offer to throw a wedding feast in the couple's honor. Some of the happiest years of Clara's life followed her marriage to Richard; she gave birth first to a son, Richard Jr., then a daughter, Margaret, and finally twin daughters, Eliza Jane and Paulina Ann.

Events took a tragic turn when Clara's twins were eight years old, however. The two girls, inseparable playmates, decided to go for a swim in a forbidden creek. As her sister watched, a strong current caught Paulina, sweeping her downstream in the rapids. Eliza Jane raced to the house, calling frantically for help. Clara sounded an alarm and rushed to the pond, where every available hand gathered in response to the cry. Richard dove into the creek again and again, searching for his daughter. Finally, his face shattered with pain, the distraught father surfaced with the body of Paulina, whose feet had become hopelessly entangled in the plants at the bottom of the river.

Eight-year-old Eliza Jane was devastated by the death of her twin sister. She blamed herself for the tragedy and regularly awoke from dreams screaming in fear. Beset with bouts of nausea and trembling, some people said Eliza Jane had lost her mind, but Clara believed her daughter would eventually be healed. Calling out for God's peace in the midst of her suffering, Clara said she felt His sustaining power. During this harrowing time, she developed a habit that would remain with her throughout her life: if she felt the need to speak with God, she dropped to her knees regardless of where she was and who might be watching. When she needed to talk to the Lord, Clara reasoned, the rest of the world could wait.[7]

Unfortunately, Paulina's death was only the first of several tragedies. Clara's mother passed away, followed by Master Smith himself. The Smith family struggled to retain the farm, but eventually they had to let it go. Though it caused them great pain, their property had to be sold to pay the bills, and unfortunately that property included Clara and her family.

On a scorching hot day in Kentucky, Clara returned to the auction block for a second time, where she, her husband, and their three children were sold to different buyers. Though the family hoped to be sold together, this was a rare phenomenon. Margaret, only a teen, was sold first as a housekeeper. Next, Richard and Richard Jr. were purchased by a man from the south with a hard, pinched face. Just looking at the man sent chills of fear down Clara's spine. Finally, ten-year-old Eliza Jane was led to the auction block in a pink pinafore, her eyes crazy with fear. Facing the crowd of strangers, the girl shook as the nausea returned, and she threw up all over her dress. Clara stepped to the stand to wipe the sick off her child's soiled pinafore with a kerchief. The trembling girl was bid upon, sold, and loaded into a wagon. As each cart pulled away from the county gathering, Clara's heart was torn in three different directions. She had no way of knowing where her husband and children were being taken, nor if she would ever see them again.

George Brown, a kind and wealthy man, purchased Clara on that sweltering day. Though devastated by the loss of her family, she called upon God to help her bear the pain, and set to work. What else could she do? Speaking of the traumatic events of her life, she later said, "Oh child, just stop and think how our Blessed Lord was crucified. Think how He suffered. My little sufferings was nothing, honey, and the Lord, He gave me strength to bear them up."[8]

As years passed, the Brown family learned to adore Clara, whom they all called "Auntie." Although Clara grew to love living with the Browns, she grieved daily for her husband and children. After a few years, she begged George Brown to seek news of her family, and he agreed. After making inquiries, George learned that Eliza Jane and Margaret were both in Kentucky. Sadly, he could not find the men. Several years later, he received word that Margaret had died of a chest ailment. In 1852, he lost track of Eliza Jane. Only four years later, George Brown passed away.

When Master Brown's will was read aloud, a shocked Clara learned he had left her three hundred dollars—the first money she had ever possessed. But even more surprising was the news that Brown's daughters wanted to set Clara free. Unfortunately, this was not an easy proposition in Kentucky at the time. In order to gain her freedom, she would have to return to the slave auctions. As long as the Browns won the bidding and Clara could pay one-quarter of the selling price, she would be free. If they lost the auction, however, Clara would remain a slave and receive a new owner. Mary Prue Brown paid $475 for Clara at auction that day; Clara contributed $118.75 of her own money, becoming a free woman at the age of fifty-six.[9]

Kentucky law gave Clara one year to leave the state or she would become a slave once more, so Clara adopted the last name of the Brown family, and boarded a flatboat bound for St. Louis.[10] In the bustling port city, she found work as a housekeeper and cook, hoping that the constant traffic through the city might bring word of her daughter. Clara knew the odds were stacked against their reunion—for one thing, she had no idea what her daughter's last name might be. Also, teaching a slave to read and write was forbidden by Kentucky law, so both women's literacy was limited. Still, Clara trusted God knew where Eliza Jane was, and she used the time in St. Louis to seek word about her daughter.

While Clara cleaned houses in St. Louis, the Supreme Court puzzled over the decision of Dred Scott. In what was later called "unquestionably, our court's worst decision ever,"[11] the Supreme Court declared Scott the property of his master. Far from settling the question of slavery as the court intended, however, the ruling unified abolitionists and only increased the fury of the debate. Most people in Missouri supported slavery, but St. Louis prided itself on being more progressive and forward thinking. But as clashes between pro- and anti-slavery groups turned violent, a new favored tactic of protest arose. It involved kidnapping freed blacks and selling them back into slavery. In a short period of time, St. Louis became a very dangerous place to be a free African-American. When some of the people Clara worked for decided to move again, she opted to accompany them to Kansas.

The discovery of gold in Colorado Territory in 1859 started a mad case of gold rush fever.[12] Almost overnight, the entire population of Leavenworth, Kansas, wanted to go west. Clara didn't care about the gold, but a thriving economy and a peaceful, tolerant community sounded enticing. Plus, the territory drew many former slaves. Clara would not let go of the elusive hope that she might hear word of her daughter at last. It had been more than twenty years since she had last seen her girl trembling on the auction block.

The journey west by wagon was expensive, though, and Clara needed to wait for the right opportunity. Ever resourceful, she reached out to Colonel Wadsworth, a respectable man leading a westward company. Clara convinced the colonel he would need a reliable cook and laundress on the migration. Blacks were not allowed in the wagons, so by day, Clara walked beside the creaking vehicles. By night, she slept on the ground under the stars. Morning, noon, and night, she prepared meals and washed dishes for the twenty-six single men in the company. It was certainly not the easiest way to travel to Colorado. Along the trail, Clara and the company faced a blizzard and a buffalo stampede, an intimidating company of Kiowa Indians, and the dangers of the desert.

Most discouraging of all, as they neared the end of the eight-week journey, the pioneers met bands of disillusioned miners traveling in the opposite direction. There was no gold, the travelers told Clara and her companions. In fact, gold hadn't been found for over a year. The whole rush was a hoax started by the outfitting companies who seemed to be the only people getting rich from the venture. Upon hearing these reports, hundreds of wagons turned around and headed for home.

Clara decided to continue. In spite of the complaints, in spite of the frequent graves that lined the stretch of trail known as "Smoky Hell," and in spite of enduring forty-eight blistering hours without fresh water, Clara never wavered. She started out intending to reach Colorado, and she didn't plan to stop until she accomplished her goal. Clara's resilience paid off when the company camped for the last night and encountered a few excited scouts heading east with encouraging news: more gold had been discovered!

After such an announcement, the arrival at Cherry Creek the next day seemed slightly anti-climactic. At the base of the Rocky Mountains, Clara found a bedraggled assortment of tepees, tents, and cabins abandoned by the discouraged miners now on their way home. The few remaining settlers were busy celebrating the discovery of a new lode of gold. Clara spent twenty-five dollars to buy an abandoned cabin, where she soon set up a thriving laundry business. As word of the discovery spread, hordes of fortune hunters descended on Cherry Creek and Denver City. The area clearly was not going to stay quiet for long, so Clara sold her cabin and moved to Central City, a mining town in the mountains high above Denver. Here, Clara bought a simple two-room cabin and reestablished her laundry business, the very first in town. No sooner had she hung up a sign when customers walked through the door, happy to pay the exorbitant price of fifty cents a shirt.[13]

Within a few short years, Clara's financial situation improved dramatically. With funds from the booming laundry business, she purchased claims in the gold and silver mines, real estate in Central City, Boulder, and Denver, and saved more than ten thousand dollars.[14] As one of the few women in Colorado to own property, Clara had become one of the wealthiest women in the West. Wealth didn't change Clara's habits that much, however. She used her money to help start the Methodist church out of her home and "adopted" many a miner in need of family and a hot meal. Still living in her two-room cabin, Clara saved most of her money, planning to travel the country if need be in search of Eliza Jane.

Before she could leave, however, Abraham Lincoln won the presidential election, and the nation plunged into civil war, which only added danger to the rough-and-tumble Colorado town. The Central City Miners' Register recorded, "We are in receipt of a communication from old Aunt Clara, than whom there is not a more respectable upright colored woman in the territory, in which she complains of some very indecent, disgraceful and insulting language addressed to her on one of our streets by some low-lived fellow who considers himself far her superior. . . . We have heard of several like instances of late."[15]

Even as men left to join the war efforts, conflict erupted closer to home. For the past several years, Arapaho and Cheyenne Indians had watched settlers stream onto their lands, shooting buffalo for pleasure until the Indians' food and clothing supply dwindled toward extinction. Initially the Indians had been promised they could keep their lands, but the discovery of gold meant the treaties were abandoned; the Indians were forced to sign a new treaty confining them to the dry and dusty desert Clara had once traveled. Angered by the deception, Indians broke into pioneer homes to steal food, clothing, and horses.

When a group of rogue braves scalped a family of farmers, the army marched in retaliation on Sand Creek Indian settlement, a settlement containing mainly women, children, and elderly, which the government had sworn to protect. Though the Indians waved white flags of surrender, soldiers used muskets and hatchets to slaughter hundreds of innocent people. Clara, whose grandmother had been full-blooded Cherokee, was heartbroken by the news. Her door had always been open to any who suffered—black, white, or native. She had hoped the settlers and the Indians would be able to find a way to live in peace.

The end of the Civil War in 1865 extinguished slavery forever, and Clara was free to travel at last. Only ten days later, rejoicing turned to mourning over the assassination of Abraham Lincoln. In spite of the unfolding chaos, Clara had waited long enough. In October, Clara sold some of her property and set out across the plains, this time heading east. Much had changed since her first journey to the territory. The stagecoach took twelve days to carry her from Denver to Kansas City, where she reunited with the Brown family and told them of her desire to find Eliza Jane. Traveling the countryside, she did not find her daughter, but she did discover thousands of freed slaves searching for their family members, in desperate need of work. Moved by the suffering, Clara adopted many who needed her help, hoping that someone, somewhere would be as kind to her own Eliza Jane.

All through the winter, Clara assisted wherever she could. By spring, she had collected somewhere between sixteen and thirty-four such wanderers,[16] and paid to equip an entire wagon train to bring the former slaves to Colorado. Every mile of the journey was familiar to Clara, and this time she ensured there was room for *everyone* to sleep in the wagons. Back in Central City, Clara helped the adoptees find jobs and homes, settling many into her own properties. Dazzled by what she had accomplished, Clara's town welcomed the newcomers with open arms. In an article called, "A Woman in a Thousand," the *Rocky Mountain News* wrote: "We will put 'Aunt Clara' against the world, white or black, for industry, perseverance, energy, and filial love."[17]

Surrounded by friends and beloved by her community, Clara remained determined to find Eliza Jane. She offered a thousand-dollar reward for word of her daughter and sent letters to churches all over the country.[18] In 1878, Clara learned that thousands of former slaves had descended on Kansas. Plenty of open land brought a steady exodus from the South, where the "exodusters" arrived without money or food and set to work building houses out of anything they could find. Lured by the hope of unfulfilled promises, many ended up sick and starving. Clara, now in her late seventies, answered the call to help, again using the trip as an opportunity to look for Eliza.

This time Clara traveled by train from Denver to Kansas City, completing the route in only two days. In camps of the sick and suffering, Clara fed the hungry and prayed over the dying. Finally, after more than a year of lending assistance, Clara returned home, still without any word of her daughter.

In the face of this last disappointment, Clara moved to Denver, feeling tired and discouraged. Her health began to fail, and it seemed the indefatigable Aunt Clara was slowing down at last. In moments of despair, Clara wondered why the Lord had not answered her one, most fervent prayer. Some of her friends began to wonder if the end drew near, but three years later, on Valentine's Day in 1882, a letter arrived. It was from a former Denver resident who had since moved to Council Bluffs, Iowa. At the post office one day, she had met a woman by the name of Eliza Jane. Could this be Clara's Eliza Jane? When questioned, this woman said she did not believe her mother could still be alive, but when asked about a drowned twin sister, Eliza Jane's eyes filled with tears.

Beside herself at the news, Clara's health made a dramatic recovery. Against doctor's orders, she insisted on traveling to Council Bluffs, though friends expressed concern that perhaps there had been some mistake. Clara was now in her eighties. Would she be able to survive the journey, much less the disappointment if this woman was not in fact her daughter? The name Eliza Jane was common enough and surely drowning was not an infrequent occurrence, but after forty-six years of praying, nothing was going to keep Clara from learning the truth. Her wealth had been exhausted over the years due to the loss of property in fires, dishonest business partners, and her unfailing generosity,[19] but friends arrived from far and wide, bringing food, clothes, and money in return for the love and kindness Clara had offered to so many over the years.

On March 3, 1882, Clara boarded the train in Denver's brand new Union Station. Just a few short days later, on a rainy, frigid morning, the conductor helped Clara descend the steps in Omaha, Nebraska; from there, she rode the streetcar across the river to Council Bluffs. Icy puddles filled the street as she stepped down and scanned the rain-darkened avenue. Someone approached, but Clara's eyesight was not what it once had been. It wasn't until the woman was right in front of her that she could see—high cheekbones like Clara's own, a smile reminiscent of Richard's, and brown eyes Clara would have recognized anywhere.

"Mammy," Eliza Jane said. Reaching for Clara, the younger woman slipped on the slick surface as Clara's hand extended for her daughter, and the two women tumbled to the ground.[20] Did the mud and wet matter to Clara? It did not. She hugged the daughter she had believed against all odds she would find. Holding each other in the mud, all that mattered to Clara was that her little girl had at last come home.

Several weeks later, Clara returned to Denver, but she did not go alone. Eliza Jane came with her, joyfully welcomed by Clara's friends and community. The *Denver Republican* wrote, "The old lady . . . has firm faith in the efficacy of prayer. She has never ceased to ask God . . . to restore her daughter to her."[21]

Clara spent the last three and a half years of her life in the company of her beloved Eliza Jane, surrounded by those she had helped in her younger years. When Clara at last passed away, the Colorado

Pioneer Association paid tribute to this remarkable woman: "Rising from the humble position of a slave to the angelic type of a noble woman, [she] won our sympathy and commanded our respect."[22]

❧

Clara's life spanned the evolution of slavery to Civil War and emancipation. She watched Indian tribes dwindle and buffalo disappear. In front of her, the rough-and-tumble frontier transformed into a string of bustling, tidy towns. To a modern world changing at a frantic pace, her steady vision in the midst of sweeping changes offers inspiration.

To me, Clara's life gives essential context to the racial tensions and divides which have not yet been resolved in the world. Seen through the prism of her experience, they become lingering vestiges of an eradicated system, though the long-term effects have proven much more challenging to eliminate. Her life reveals the overwhelming roadblocks faced by those who struggled against the institution of slavery: the debilitating effects of illiteracy, the fracturing of families, and the systematic oppression and control of power.

It is difficult to imagine a more impossible set of odds than the ones faced by Clara. The graciousness with which she lifted herself above these odds and then turned bitterness into generosity offers hope to all of us who suffer in desperate circumstances. Against the depravity of prejudice, Clara pitted hard work, grit, and intelligence and rose to success. In that success, she found others in need of love and care. To wealthy or poor, black or white, there was always something she could give.

This is not to imply that racial prejudice is not real and systematic changes are not needed; it is simply the realization that each of us have more control over our own actions than we do over the circumstances in which we are born. Clara used anguish and pain from oppression to fuel some of her life's greatest accomplishments, channeling hurt into acts of love rather than acts of violence.

Perhaps the most remarkable part of Clara Brown's story is the fact that through the repeated disappointments of passing years, in spite of staggering odds and the well-meaning discouragement of those who urged her to be more realistic, Clara chose to hold on to hope and faith. To me, her story says that no dream is ever too late, no hope ever truly impossible. Some dreams are worth holding on to, even if they take forty-six years to come true.

FURTHER READING

Kathleen Bruyn, *"Aunt" Clara Brown: Story of a Black Pioneer* (Boulder, CO: Pruett Publishing Co., 1970).

William Loren Katz, *The Black West* (New York: Touchstone, 1996).

William Loren Katz, *Black Women of the Old West* (New York: Atheneum, 1995).

Linda Lowery, *One More Valley, One More Hill: The Story of Aunt Clara Brown* (New York: Random House, 2002).

NOTES

1. Linda Lowery, *One More Valley, One More Hill: The Story of Aunt Clara Brown* (New York: Random House, 2002), 203.
2. Dred Scott v. Sandford, 60 U.S. 19 Howard 393 (1856). Accessed online at https://supreme.justia .com/cases/federal/us/60/393/case.html.
3. William Loren Katz, *Black Women of the Old West* (New York: Atheneum, 1995), 24.
4. See Lowery, *One More Valley*.
5. Kathleen Bruyn, *"Aunt" Clara Brown: Story of a Black Pioneer* (Boulder, CO: Pruett Publishing Co., 1970), 5.
6. Lowery, *One More Valley*, 204.
7. Bruyn, *"Aunt" Clara Brown*, 8.
8. Lowery, *One More Valley*, 204.
9. Ibid., 34.
10. Katz, *Black Women of the Old West*, 24.
11. David Konig et al., *The Dred Scott Case: Historical and Contemporary Perspectives on Race and Law* (Ohio University Press, 2010), 213. Accessed online at http://www.ohioswallow.com/book /The+Dred+Scott+Case.
12. Katz, *Black Women of the Old West*, 24.
13. William Loren Katz, *The Black West* (New York: Touchstone, 1996), 78.
14. Ibid.

15. Lowery, *One More Valley*, 142.

16. Accounts differ regarding the number of people who returned with Clara. Katz claims it was thirty-four, but Lowery in *One More Valley*, 168, says other historians believe it was fewer. Regardless, those who returned with Clara considered themselves greatly blessed by her kindness and generosity.

17. Lowery, *One More Valley*, 169.

18. Katz, *Black Women of the Old West*, 25.

19. Clara lost quite a bit of property when records kept at the Central City courthouse, which contained deeds of sale, burned in the fire of 1874. She was also swindled by the person who outfitted her company for the journey west the second time. For more information, see Bruyn, *"Aunt" Clara Brown: Story of a Black Pioneer*, 148.

20. Accounts differ regarding who fell first—mother or daughter. One way or another, they both ended up in the mud, oblivious to their surroundings, overcome with joy.

21. Lowery, *One More Valley*, 172.

22. Ibid., 203.

CHAPTER 3

ABIGAIL SCOTT DUNIWAY
OREGON TRAIL SUFFRAGETTE

Born: October 22, 1834, Groveland, Illinois
Died: October 11, 1915, Portland, Oregon

"The young college women of today—free to study, to speak, to write, to choose their occupation, should remember that every inch of this freedom was bought for them at a great price."[1]

At the auspicious age of six, Abigail Scott gathered the village children of Groveland, Illinois, beneath the sturdy branches of a sycamore tree. Climbing nimbly onto a horizontal branch, she "harangued them" for some time with her political views (mainly adopted from her father) on the current candidates for United States president.[2] No remaining records indicate the reaction of her young audience, but it's unlikely any of the small admirers appreciated that they were witnessing the first of thousands of political speeches Abigail would deliver over the course of her life.

As soon as Abigail, called Jenny by family and friends, learned to read, her favorite texts became the popular newspapers, the rough equivalent of the Internet social networks of today. In isolated frontier towns, newspapers carried coveted local, national, and international intelligence, but they also carried poetry, fiction, opinion pieces, and local gossip. Public debate and discussion filled the pages, particularly the "Letter to the Editor" section.

A young preacher lived with Abigail's family during her early teenage years and he introduced her to the *New York Tribune.* Though Abigail's father initially opposed the "radical" paper, Abigail found every opportunity to "purloin it from his table, and peruse it regularly."[3] Eventually her father warmed up to the publication, and young Abigail and her sisters devoured the content, participating vicariously in the debates over slavery and the newly created Convention on Women's Rights. Years later, Abigail would claim the editor of the *Tribune,* Horace Greeley, had "done more to shape our destiny than that of any other living intelligence."[4] The *Tribune* offered a window through which young Abigail could gaze upon a world of ideas expressed in printed form—a debate over the future of a developing nation.

Fascinated by the power of printed letters, Abigail nurtured dreams of one day becoming a writer. Greeley's advice on the subject influenced her deeply: "When a mind crowded with discovered or elaborated truths *will* have utterance, begin to write sparingly and tersely for the nearest suitable periodical—no matter how humble and obscure—if the thought is in you, it will find its way to those who need it."[5] Greeley's advice inspired the budding young wordsmith, who immediately began writing poems and sending them out for publication. Decades later, Abigail would indeed brandish the power of her pen on behalf of those who needed it.

Far too little of Abigail's childhood involved intellectual pursuits for her liking, however. When she was born in an Illinois log cabin, her parents' sorrow at having a girl instead of the male heir they desired was "almost too grievous to be born."[6] As the second surviving child followed by nine subsequent siblings, Abigail found that life on the frontier involved harsh, endless work, leaving precious little time for scribbling in notebooks. One of Abigail's earliest memories was balancing on a chair to reach a tall stack of dirty dishes in need of washing. Daily chores included milking cows, making butter, planting crops, chopping wood, and collecting sap for maple syrup. Her least favorite job was spinning and spooling wool into thread for the family's clothing. The constant physical labor left Abigail frequently ill, though in some ways the sickness turned out to be a blessing. While her sisters stayed home to work, Abigail spent a few precious months at school in Pleasant Grove and five additional months in an academy at the age of sixteen. *Webster's Elementary Spelling* book became one of her prized possessions, and she devoured the novels of Charles Dickens, whose plots filled her with a desire to right the world's wrongs.

The sorrow Abigail's parents felt at her birth turned to rejoicing three years later when her brother Harvey joined the family; the son they had longed for was given every advantage. These two strong-willed siblings competed constantly—in wrestling matches when they were younger, and in intellectual sparring sessions as they grew. To Abigail, it was a matter of blatant injustice when Harvey excused himself from household chores to receive the best education due to the benefit of his gender. She both resented and loved her younger brother.

Only a few hundred feet from the Scotts' log cabin, a rough dirt road stretched away to the west. Each spring and summer, heavily laden wagons bound for Oregon passed the family's home. Intrigued by tales of rivers brimming with salmon, snow-capped volcanoes, and lush, rich farmland for the taking, Abigail's father, Tucker Scott, grew enchanted by the idea of going west. Abigail's mother, Ann, who had just endured her twelfth childbirth and the death of that baby, opposed the move, but Tucker insisted, claiming the new environment would be good for Ann's health. He sold the farm and all their belongings at auction and informed Abigail that all books would be left behind. She smuggled her beloved spelling book by hiding it at the bottom of her sewing basket, however, and it was not the only forbidden item in the wagon. When sister Fanny's suitor bought the family's set of dishes at auction as a farewell present, the girls sewed the dishes inside a feather bed without their father's knowledge.

The family bid a permanent good-bye to grandparents and friends and embarked on the two-thousand-mile journey to Oregon. Tucker Scott organized his nine children for the expedition, assigning each of them particular tasks. The older girls (Fanny, Maggie, and Kitty) were responsible for the cooking and washing; Harvey drove a wagon, and Etty, age eleven, rounded up stray cattle on her pony. The little ones (John, Sarah, and Willie) helped with small chores in camp, but Abigail felt the best job of all fell to her. Tucker requested Abigail to keep a diary of their journey, presenting her with a special leather-spined ledger[7] for the work. Instructed to record their daily mileage and location, Abigail couldn't help including her own observations on the "blue tinged timber in the distance, the wild flowers and shrubs beneath our feet," which she declared, "picturesque and sublime."[8] The early stages of the journey seemed an adventure, and Abigail wrote to her grandfather: "I never enjoyed myself so well before and never had as good health before in my life. . . . No one knows what he can endure until he undertakes it."[9]

Unfortunately, the remainder of the trip called the family to endure far more than any of them could have imagined. Record numbers of emigrants headed west in 1852, taxing the trail's resources. Feed and water for cattle grew scarce, while goods were overpriced and difficult to come by. Cramped trail conditions led to the spread of disease, and the dreaded cholera stalked many of the companies. Two months into the journey, Abigail fell ill, and her mother slept by her side, caring for her throughout the night. In the morning, Ann confided that she also felt poorly. By that afternoon, Ann Scott lay dead from cholera. The family scratched a grave from sandstone and covered her body with a feather bed, rocks, and roses. Tucker

Scott could not write of his grief, so it was up to Abigail to inform the family at home.

More challenges lay ahead. Cattle died, a cousin drowned in a river, the girls' shoes gave out, food grew scarce, and nearly everyone in the company fell ill. Three-year-old Willie suffered for nine days before joining his mother in death. Willie was everyone's darling; Abigail called him "the treasure of our hearts" and mourned deeply for the child.[10] Arriving in The Dalles, Tucker used the last of their money to buy shoes for the girls. At the end of September, they reached Oregon City—hungry, grieving, and broke. The journey had been horrific, but years later a fellow pioneer conjectured it created a resilience in the Scott children they would not have otherwise developed. "Where else would daughters [like Abigail Scott Duniway] develop the determination to win a fight for a principle, lasting through two generations, than in that plodding, toilsome journey?"[11]

Anxious to put the agonies of the trail behind him, Tucker Scott began a farm and a boardinghouse, while Abigail took a job teaching school using the very Webster speller she had smuggled across the plains. For her work, she was paid half as much as the male teachers.[12] Though she may have been underappreciated in the work force, a severe shortage of women in Oregon at that time, combined with land incentives for marrying, left Abigail surrounded by suitors. She refused to marry someone for the financial benefits but fell in love with the generous and handsome rancher Ben Duniway. Insisting the word "obey" be omitted from their wedding vows, Abigail married Ben, and the two settled on land south of Oregon City.

Over the next several years, Abigail found herself reliving her mother's life, something she had never planned to do. Isolated on a farm, she made butter, soap, and quilts, and gave birth to babies (six eventually) in fairly quick succession. She adored her children, but a move to the township of Lafayette gave Abigail more opportunities to socialize and renew her literary hopes. In 1859, her book *Captain Gray's Company, or Crossing the Plains and Living in Oregon* became the first commercially printed novel in Oregon. One reviewer wrote, "It is a sad, sad story, and we congratulate Mrs. Duniway upon having got rid of it."[13] Though the book received poor reviews and Abigail herself acknowledged its defects, the thrill of seeing her name in print fueled her continued writing endeavors.

The farm's profitability enabled Abigail to write, but in 1861, Ben's generous nature moved him to help a friend by cosigning his loan notes. With a large harvest stored in a warehouse, it seemed a safe enough move. Abigail expressed concerns, though as a woman she legally did not have a say in the matter. Ben reassured her, "Mama, you needn't worry; you'll always be protected and provided for!"[14] However, flooding destroyed their storehouse of wheat before it could be sold. Ben tried to rescue their finances by working in a mine, but eventually they were forced to sell the farm.

The impoverished family retreated to town, where Abigail opened a school. Further disaster unfolded when a heavily loaded wagon struck Ben down in the street, leaving him unable to work. Abigail became the main supporter of her family while Ben looked after the children and home. The new situation was in some ways a better match for their temperaments, as Ben loved children and Abigail's ambitious nature reveled in industry. She purchased supplies to open a millinery and notions shop and soon conducted a brisk business.

Abigail started the shop to support her family, but the storefront soon became a gathering place for countless women to find support in their struggles. One customer's husband sold all their belongings and left town, abandoning his wife and children. Heartbroken, the woman begged Abigail for money to borrow to open a boardinghouse. Though Abigail arranged a loan, months later, the husband returned and rejected the mortgage, which was legally invalid without his signature. He sold the furniture at auction and pocketed the proceeds, then took the children and divorced his wife. Another of Abigail's customers sold butter and saved for months to buy new coats for her children. Just before making the purchase, her husband used the funds to buy a new racehorse instead. Abigail burned at these injustices. Women contributed economically, were held accountable for debts, but remained powerless to own property or manage their own incomes.

Once while she was helping a friend through a difficult legal proceeding, Abigail was told by a judge, "Of course, being ladies, you wouldn't be expected to understand the intricacies of the law." Abigail retorted, "No, but we are expected to know enough to foot the bills."[15] At night she recounted her experience to Ben, complaining about yet another man who was "heartless enough to act toward his family as the law permits." Ben responded, "Don't you know it will never be any better for women until they have the right to vote?"[16]

Abigail described that moment as her "third birth." She realized that Ben was right. If women had the right to vote, they could become lawmakers and shape more equitable legislation. Now the mother of six, Abigail started the State Equal Suffrage Association in 1870 with two of her closest friends. By this time, younger brother Harvey had graduated from Pacific Univiersity and landed a prestigious job as editor of *The Oregonian*. Although Abigail submitted articles on the topic of suffrage to Harvey for publication, he repeatedly turned them down, fueling a continuation of the sibling rivalry that had long existed between them. Clearly Portland needed a new perspective, one that would herald the cause of women's rights. Never one to waste time, Abigail moved her family to Portland, turned the millinery business over to her oldest daughter, Clara, and bought a printing press and type. Abigail's sons already worked in various parts of the news industry, so she hired a typesetter and put her sons to work learning additional aspects of the trade.

In the first issue of *The New Northwest,* Abigail included a serialized story, poems from local authors, a fashion column, news and gossip, and a searing attack on three prominent women who had recently spoken out against women's rights. On the topic of fashion, Abigail wrote: "A trailing dress is an emblem of degradation. It is suggestive of weak brain and back aches; of dependence and incompetency; of frailty and subjugation."[17] In the health section, she counseled readers, "The best remedy for 'nerves' that we ever tried was 'lots' of active and absorbing business."[18]

The paper, with its snarky, fearless voice, created an immediate sensation. The publication carried the pithy motto: "A Journal for the People Devoted to the Interests of Humanity Independent in Politics and Religion Alive to All Live Issues and Thoroughly Radical in Opposing and Exposing the Wrongs of the Masses."[19] Over the next sixteen years, *The New Northwest* became the heart of the women's movement in Portland. Reporting on cultural and political events, investigating asylums and prisons, defending the maligned and attacking the fraudulent, Abigail mentored hundreds of women, encouraging them to seek education, find a voice, and improve the laws of the country.

Shortly after starting the paper, Abigail estimated it would take five years for female suffrage to pass in Oregon. She invited Susan B. Anthony and Elizabeth Cady Stanton to give a series of lectures in the region. To her delight, Susan B. Anthony accepted, and Abigail joined her for a two-month lecture tour. Anthony described Abigail as "a sprightly, intelligent, young woman. . . . her husband—a sensible man—is proud that his wife possesses brains and self-respect to use them."[20] Embarking on the tour as an inexperienced public speaker, Abigail discovered that people enjoyed her feisty, engaging style, and the lectures were soon in great demand. Susan and Abigail spoke at state fairs, schools, churches, and private homes, and even addressed a session at the territorial legislature in Olympia, Washington.

The speaking tour gained supporters as well as enemies. Some accused the women of "selling out to whiskey"[21]; others insisted universal suffrage would bring "divisions in homes, anarchy in families" and "destroy all that is pure and beautiful in human nature."[22] In Jacksonville, Oregon, opponents threw eggs at the "radical" women. Abigail reported, "Only one egg hit us, and that was fresh and sweet, and it took us square on the scalp and saved a shampooing bill."[23] One of the most powerful opponents of the female vote in Oregon remained Abigail's lifelong rival, her brother Harvey. Believing uneducated voters to be dangerous, *The Oregonian* editorials reflected his positions, which of course enraged Abigail, and their verbal disputes at family gatherings became notorious.

Though female suffrage remained elusive, Abigail began to see some success. Oregon passed a law giving women the right to own property and wages independent of their husbands, and The Sole Trader Bill helped women avoid having their property seized by their husband's creditors. In 1883, twelve years after she had started her paper, Abigail witnessed the Washington Territory legislature give the final "aye" in favor of women's suffrage. She raced to telegraph the news to her sons, who published the breaking news as a last-minute update. Abigail hoped Oregon wouldn't be far behind. Working tirelessly toward this goal, her records from 1886 indicate that she traveled 3,000 miles, delivered 181 lectures, penned 400 columns, and attended the national suffrage convention.[24]

Unfortunately, roadblocks still lay ahead. In a disappointing reversal, the state of Washington cancelled women's suffrage due to prohibition, and Abigail came under attack from others in the movement who disagreed with her stance on alcohol. Many suffragists supported the prohibition on alcohol, and the two platforms joined forces, though Abigail felt it was dangerous to combine the two issues. Her enemies exploited the position and called her a supporter of alcoholic vice and corruption. During one of Abigail's lectures, a group of opponents repeatedly stood up and started singing every time she began to speak. After a few obstructed attempts to speak, Abigail finally declared: "Let us pray," and delivered her speech in the form of prayer instead. In a lengthy invocation, she explained to the Lord why suffrage was so essential, using a delivery method no one present dared to interrupt.[25]

The difficult times extended to Abigail's personal life as well. Her oldest daughter, Clara, grew ill and died from tuberculosis. In a final blow, Ben and their sons decided to buy a ranch in Idaho, forcing Abigail to sell her paper in 1887. She said it was like "parting with a loved and trusted child."[26] The Idaho ranch did not succeed, however, and eventually the family returned to Portland. Abigail continued to wax prolific, as novels, poetry, and newspaper articles flowed from her pen. She continued lecturing widely on the topics of women's rights and suffrage. Idaho adopted suffrage in 1896, the same year that Ben passed away. Abigail paid tribute to him as both a wonderful husband and a tireless supporter of women's causes.

Though most other western states had by this time adopted female suffrage laws, the movement languished in Oregon due to opposition from liquor businesses and the influence of *The Oregonian*. Abigail's five-year prediction for suffrage had turned into forty. Though happily occupied with grandchildren, she did not want to leave the earth without seeing the accomplishment of her goal. Abigail prepared carefully for the election of 1900 by refusing help from national organizers and writing countless letters to influential businessmen, persuading them that prohibition should be unrelated. After an awful confrontation at a family birthday party, Harvey Scott promised not to stand in her way; with his agreement, Abigail felt sure the measure would pass. But two weeks before the election, Harvey went "out of town" and conveniently could not be reached, while *The Oregonian* launched a massive attack against the amendment. The interests of the liquor companies reigned once more, and the measure failed by 2,000 votes. When an abashed Harvey reappeared, Abigail gave him a tongue-lashing he would not soon forget.[27]

Astoundingly, the measure failed again in 1906, 1908, and 1910; in fact, Oregon voted on the issue of women's suffrage more times than any other state. In several elections, blatant abuse surfaced, such as the marked ballots sent by the Brewer's and Wholesale Liquor Dealers' Association to every liquor retailer in the state; in another, votes were purchased for $2.50 apiece.[28] After the continued losses, Abigail's sons advised their mother to let the suffrage issue go. Now in her mid-seventies, she suffered from increasingly poor health, but her pen would not be stopped. She continued the plea she had maintained for forty years: "The mother half of all the people is rated in law with idiots, insane persons and criminals, from whose legal classification we are looking to you, voters of Oregon, to release us,"[29] she implored.

Harvey's death in 1910 finally brought the opposition of *The Oregonian* to an end. Abigail personally obtained petitions and submitted the amendment in the 1912 election. Suffering from a painful leg infection, Abigail continued directing the campaign from her bed. In October, she celebrated her seventy-eighth birthday with a formal banquet attended by Governor Oswald West. Yellow decorations, the color associated with suffrage, reminded all attendees of

Abigail's life work. On the night of the election, while other supporters stayed up late, Abigail went to bed in case she needed to begin a new campaign in the morning. The sounds of a joyous parade awakened her, however. Suffrage had passed by a narrow margin. Women in the state of Oregon could vote at last.

Governor West had first heard Abigail speak on behalf of women's rights at a state fair when he was just a boy. He had never forgotten the speech, which moved him deeply. Now tasked with the creation of a Suffrage Amendment, the governor called upon Abigail to write and sign the Proclamation. She spent three days handwriting the document,[30] which the governor signed in her presence. He invited Abigail to be the first woman registered to vote and the first female voter in Multnomah County. When Abigail arrived at the polls, the registrar asked the seventy-eight-year-old woman if he should list her occupation as "retired." She responded, "I am not retired yet. . . . I am still working to the best of my ability to bring equal suffrage to every part of the United States."[31]

In an interview shortly after the victory, Abigail said, "I think that now we have the ballot, we all should make use of it."[32] This remarkable woman passed away five years before the Nineteenth Constitutional Amendment granted suffrage to all U.S. women. She spent her last few years writing an autobiography entitled *Path Breaking*, which concludes: "The young college women of today— free to study, to speak, to write, to choose their occupation, should remember that every inch of this freedom was bought for them at a great price. It is for them to show their gratitude by helping onward the reforms of their own time, by spreading the light of freedom and of truth still wider. The debt that each generation owes to the past it must pay to the future."[33] The words truly reflect the greatness of her life—a fitting benediction for all that she lived for.

Abigail faced a world of tough and even violent strife, and stood amidst the conflict, brandishing the power of her pen. Without a fancy degree or the comfort of wealth, she dared to believe her own voice was important. She dared to do the work she felt called upon to do. Armed with a strong personality and a fiery temper, she was bound to find enemies for her controversial views, but she didn't let opposition dissuade her from what she believed was best for the future of her city, state, and nation.

∞

While doing research for this chapter, I visited the Oregon Historical Society and handled volumes of ledgers painstakingly set out in the ink of Abigail's elegant cursive. The magnitude of this collection is overwhelming—boxes of letters, columns, and minutes from meetings testify of her devotion to the cause, of her tireless work in behalf of future generations of women. Even the letterhead of an envelope, yellowed and faded with time, reminded recipients of her stance:

Oregon State Equal Suffrage Assoc.

Mrs. Abigail Scott Duniway, Pres.

Women Pay Taxes, Women Should Vote

Though influencing the collective thought of a nation may seem by turns overwhelming, discouraging, and hopeless, Abigail's efforts are motivation to stay involved regardless—reminding us that the world will be marginally less corrupt if *we* refuse to be corrupted. The span of history that separates the present from Abigail's time has exonerated her positions—prohibition eventually failed and suffrage did indeed become universal. In spite of dissension from the most influential powers of her day, she maintained her course. The issues themselves are perhaps less important than the pattern. Do not doubt that thoughtful, intelligent people can still draw conclusions far ahead of broader society. Abigail is a resounding reminder not to minimize your own opinions nor doubt the power of your voice to truly change the world.

FURTHER READING

Abigail Scott Duniway, *Path Breaking: An Autobiographical History of the Equal Suffrage Movement in Pacific Coast States* (Portland, OR: James, Kerns, and Abbott, 1914).

Dorothy Nafus Morrison, *Ladies Were Not Expected: Abigail Scott Duniway and Women's Rights* (New York: Atheneum, 1977).

Ruth Barnes Moynihan, *Rebel for Rights: Abigail Scott Duniway* (New Haven, CT: Yale University Press, 1983).

Yours for Liberty: Selections from Abigail Scott Duniway's Suffrage Newspaper, edited by Jean M. Ward and Elaine A. Maveety (Corvallis: Oregon State University Press, 2000).

NOTES

1. Abigail Scott Duniway, *Path Breaking: An Autobiographical History of the Equal Suffrage Movement in Pacific Coast States* (Portland, OR: James, Kerns, and Abbott, 1914), 297.

2. Ibid., 5.

3. Dorothy Nafus Morrison, *Ladies Were Not Expected: Abigail Scott Duniway and Women's Rights* (New York: Atheneum, 1977), 12.

4. *The New Northwest,* June 30, 1871, in *Yours for Liberty: Selections from Abigail Scott Duniway's Suffrage Newspaper,* edited by Jean M. Ward and Elaine A. Maveety (Corvallis: Oregon State University Press, 2000), 46.

5. Ruth Barnes Moynihan, *Rebel for Rights: Abigail Scott Duniway* (New Haven, CT: Yale University Press, 1983), 11.

6. Duniway, *Path Breaking,* 3.

7. Kenneth L. Holmes and David C. Duniway, *Covered Wagon Women: Diaries and Letters from the Western Trails 1840–1890* (Glendale, CA: Arthur H. Clark Company, 1986).

8. Abigail Scott Duniway Diary, 30 April 1852. Accessed online at http://oregondigital.org/catalog/oregondigital:df67wp617.

9. Moynihan, *Rebel for Rights,* 33.

10. Ibid., 39.

11. Ibid., 42.

12. Fred Lockley, *Visionaries, Mountain Men, and Empire Builders* (Eugene, OR: Rainy Day Press, 1982), 295.

13. *New York Graphic,* December 16, 1876.

14. Moynihan, *Rebel for Rights,* 68.

15. John Terry, "Duniway Broke Path for Oregon Women, Oregon Historical Society," *The Oregonian,* June 28, 1993.

16. Moynihan, *Rebel for Rights,* 82.

17. *The New Northwest,* April 12, 1872, in *Yours for Liberty,* 66.

18. *The New Northwest,* July 28, 1871, in *Yours for Liberty,* 47.

19. Moynihan, *Rebel for Rights,* 90.

20. Morrison, *Ladies Were Not Expected,* 86.

21. Karen Surina Mulford, *Trailblazers: Twenty Amazing Western Women* (Flagstaff, AZ: Northland Publishing, 2001), 37.

22. Morrison, *Ladies Were Not Expected,* 90.

23. *The New Northwest,* July 17, 1879, in *Yours for Liberty,* 185.

24. "The Register Guard 'Patchwork Legacy,'" *Oregon Life,* March 9, 1997.

25. Morrison, *Ladies Were Not Expected,* 111.

26. Moynihan, *Rebel for Rights,* 147.

27. John Terry, "Sibling Warfare," *The Oregonian,* December 14, 2003.

28. Ruth Barnes Moynihan, "Of Women's Rights and Freedom: Abigail Scott Duniway," in Karen J. Blair, ed., *Women in Pacific Northwest History* (Seattle: University of Washington Press, 1990), 28.

29. "Declaration of Principles of the Oregon State Equal Suffrage Association for Campaign of 1908," document available at Oregon Historical Society.

30. *Oregon Life,* March 9, 1997.

31. Moynihan, *Rebel for Rights,* 216.

32. "Gay Lombard and Mrs. Duniway Visit Oregon Historical Society," *The Morning Oregonian,* March 12, 1913.

33. Duniway, *Path Breaking,* 297.

CHAPTER 4

MARÍA AMPARO RUIZ DE BURTON
FIRST MEXICAN-AMERICAN FEMALE NOVELIST

Born: July 3, 1832, Loreto, Baja California, Mexico
Died: August 12, 1895, Chicago, Illinois

"Remember that I am a woman . . . and Mexican . . . with my soul enclosed in an iron cage. In this manner Society confines us as soon as we are born."[1]

The United States contains myriad borders, where varying perspectives meet and at times clash, including lines of demarcation along religious, socioeconomic, and racial differences. Daring to love across such lines is deemed an act of courage, an act fraught with danger, as represented by numerous love songs and literary archetypes, including Romeo and Juliet. The tale of star-crossed lovers from feuding families is one whose origins reach back to antiquity, far predating Shakespeare: two young lovers find themselves separated by the wall of violence established between their families. Versions of the story exist in many languages, with many variations, but nearly every iteration of *Romeo and Juliet* ends with the death of the protagonists, demonstrating the real risks of such a connection. The concept of borders and the courage to love across them is central to the life and work of María Amparo Ruiz de Burton—she explored the theme in novel form, but she lived it as well.

The western boundaries of the United States did a great deal of shifting in the 1800s. In the early part of the century, the western border stretched from Wisconsin in the north to Louisiana in the south. When settlers established colonies in Texas, California, New

Mexico, Nevada, Utah, and Arizona, they did so in Mexican territory. While the American Revolutionary War concluded in 1776, Mexico declared its freedom from the colonial power of Spain in 1821. The first few decades were difficult ones as the sovereign nation worked out details of a new government. Mexico was still on shaky ground when American settlers in Texas declared independence, establishing the Texas Republic in 1835. Ten years later, the United States annexed Texas, leading to the eruption of the Mexican-American War, or as it is called in Mexico, *Invasión Estadounidense a México* (United States's Invasion of Mexico). U.S. troops marched from Washington, D.C., to Mexico City, forcing the new Mexican government to surrender in 1847. The peace agreement compelled Mexico to sell what is now modern-day California, Texas, Arizona, New Mexico, and Nevada—fully half of Mexico's territory—to the United States for fifteen million dollars.[2] The discovery of gold took place in California two years after the agreement. It's astounding to consider how the economies of the two nations would be different today if the boundaries had remained unchanged.

Into the midst of these tumultuous times, María Amparo Ruiz entered the world, born to a prestigious family of Spanish descent in Baja California. María's grandfather, José Manuel Ruiz, assisted with the founding of Catholic missions in the region and served as governor of the Baja region until 1825.[3] She was related to many influential families in the area and was heir to her grandfather's property—48,000 acres in Ensenada. In Maria's childhood, a flood forced her family to move from Loreto to La Paz, a small town sheltered by verdant mountains, situated on the emerald waters of the Sea of Cortez, partway down the Baja Peninsula. Although the Amparo family was not wealthy, they had a great deal of land and political clout. As evidenced from her later writings, María studied Spanish, French, literature, and European and American history, and she received education from Franciscan friars as well as a private *pro-fesora* from Spain.

The U.S. Army invaded the Baja at the same time troops in the east marched upon Mexico City. The invading soldiers included a handsome twenty-eight-year-old lieutenant colonel,[4] Henry S. Burton. Sixteen-year-old María watched the surrender of La Paz and aided the wounded at a local hospital. Her service there is thought to have inspired the lyrics for the ballad "The Maid of Monterey," which reads in part:

> *The guns had hushed their thunder*
> *The guns in silence lay*
> *Then came the señorita*
> *the Maid of Monterey.*
> *She cast a look of anguish*
> *on the dying and the dead*
> *and made her lap a pillow*
> *for those who mourned and bled.*[5]

Though a local *ranchero* had been pursuing María, she and Captain Henry Burton were smitten with each other upon their first encounter. The romance threw the community and the Ruiz family into chaos, as María was the adored daughter of the people Burton had come to conquer. Even more problematic in some ways was the fact that her family was staunchly Catholic, while Burton identified as Protestant.

As part of the Treaty of Guadalupe Hidalgo, Mexican citizens in the newly acquired U.S. lands had one year to decide if they wanted to remain in Mexico or become United States citizens. María, along with her mother and brother, rode the transport *Lexington* to Monterey in Alta, California—a convenience personally arranged by Captain Burton. In Monterey, María enrolled in language school, where she mastered English and attempted to work out the knotty details of her intended marriage to Henry. When her previously rejected suitor learned from family servants that María intended to marry the captain, he reported this news to the Bishop of California, saying, "a Catholic should not marry a Protestant."[6] The bishop agreed with the suitor, as did the newly appointed governor of California, none of which encouraged María to reconsider her choice.

In the end, María and Henry were married in 1849 by a Presbyterian minister.[7] A contemporary source remarked, "A dispensation from the Pope will be necessary before the lady can be recognized as a married woman. At present she is banished from Catholic society." Eventually local authorities rewrote the laws in order to have the marriage recognized, and the couple began life together, attempting to use the strength of their love to bridge two languages, cultures, and political structures. This is the first recorded indication that even at the age of sixteen, María did not mind flaunting predominant public opinions—it would not be the last.

During the four years they spent in Monterey, María became fluent in English; with the scandal of their marriage behind them, the couple entered society. Now married to a West Point officer, María found herself part of elite white society, but she recognized she was also separate and distinct as a *California* (the feminized term for the original Mexican inhabitants of the area). She formed friendships with writers and the literarily inclined, but she recognized that as a woman with literary aspirations, her gender set her apart. María became close friends with Don Mariano Guadalupe Vallejo of Sonoma, a wealthy *ranchero*. They both shared a love for books, and Don Mariano allowed María access to his extensive library. He praised her as "a learned and cultured lady, concerned with the honor and traditions of her land, worthy wife, loving mother and loyal friend."[8]

But the contradictory forces at play in María's life also led Vallejo to refer to her as an *"alma atravesada"*—a phrase that literally translates as "a soul that has crossed over," though *"atravesada"* also contains implications of something that is blocked or fragmented—signifying María's evolving identity that spanned two nations, pulling her in opposing directions. The phrase simultaneously connotes that she had a contrary nature and didn't mind breaking with social norms.

María knew that society would not view positively the biracial children her marriage would produce, but she chose to see the combination as an asset, a positive result of choosing to love across borders. She wrote, "The mixture of [the blood in both races] can do no less than produce a third, more beautiful, more energetic, stronger, sweet in character, more temperate, and, I believe, stronger."[9] On July 4, 1850, she gave birth to a daughter named Nellie, and four years later, her son, Henry, was born in San Diego, where the family had been transferred.

The couple homesteaded in an adobe house on Rancho Jamul, a property that included 562,000 acres outside of San Diego. The land title had a complicated and hazy history involving lost documentation and abandonment, details that created problems in years to come. The Burtons ran cattle and produced lime from limestone on the property; they became known for their lavish hospitality in the community.

In 1855, the couple started a theater company at the Mission San Diego. Here, María finally had her first opportunity to demonstrate her literary talents. The theater company performed a series of plays written by María, including a five-act comic retelling of Cervantes's *Don Quixote,* which she later had published in San Francisco.[10] This early work offers a taste of the biting political satire for which she would become known. She portrays Don Quixote fighting against corrupt lawyers and judges—enemies she herself would spend many years combating. In one scene, two judges compete to see who can best bray like a donkey. At the conclusion of this contest, one man remarks, "I can tell you, friend, that between you and an ass, there's no difference as far as braying goes, for I never in all my life heard anything more natural."[11]

In 1859, Henry traveled east to prepare for the increasing possibility of American civil war. Extended family remained behind to maintain the ranch property against the threat of squatters, who frequently attempted to steal ranch lands. María and her family traveled by steamer through the Panama Canal to Fort Monroe, Virginia, where Henry became a brigadier general in the Union army.

María began circulating in elite East Coast society—and soon she became known for her intelligence and strong opinions. The Burtons attended the inauguration of Abraham Lincoln, and María recorded, "Well, the inauguration of Mr. Lincoln has passed without problem and he has given his first public reception without having been assassinated as was expected. . . . The state of the country continues in agitation and the danger of war is ever present."[12] María became close friends with Mary Todd Lincoln. In Washington, she witnessed the inner workings of political and military life, including the scandals and corruption she would later explore in fiction.

As María anticipated, civil war did indeed break out in 1861, and the family was transferred to posts several times throughout the war, including Staten Island; Washington, D.C.; and Vermont. Her glittering rise through society came to an abrupt halt when Henry erected works around Petersburg, Virginia, a service that left him with malaria. Recurrent attacks plagued him for the next four years, and in 1869, he died, leaving María, a thirty-seven-year-old widow, with two children. She wrote to a friend, "Now I am both father and mother of my children; I am surrounded by difficulties, with God knows what for support, and even though God is good and powerful, the human heart always searches and yearns for some other support here on earth."[13]

In the midst of grief, she turned to writing as a source of protest and healing. Published anonymously three years after her husband's death, *Who Would Have Thought It?*[14] became her first novel. With wit and satire, the book critiques social norms with phrases reminiscent of Jane Austen, though with a darker, more biting tone. Set against the backdrop of the Civil War, the book tells the story of Lola, a girl of Spanish descent born into Indian captivity. Her dying mother entrusts the girl to the care of a white doctor from the east, asking him to raise the child as a Catholic and providing wealth in the form of jewels for the girl's inheritance. Dr. Norval brings the girl to his home, where his wife, who claims to be an abolitionist, is repulsed by her dark skin. Ignoring Lola's presence, Mrs. Norval asks, "How old is she? Her face is so black that truly, it baffles all my efforts to guess her age." Her much more compassionate husband responds: "She is only ten years old; but her history is already more romantic than that of half of the heroines of your trashy novels."

When Dr. Norval travels for work, Mrs. Norval uses his absence to improve her own social standing by extorting Lola's fortune; her entire character acts as a scathing denunciation of the hypocrisy of America's elite. Mrs. Norval's rejection of Lola, combined with her willingness to profit from her fortune is interpreted as an allegorical reference to the United States' willingness to seize land from Mexico while simultaneously rejecting the Mexican people and their culture. In the novel, Minister Hackwell uses his religious office to gain wealth and engage in sexual exploits, illustrating that too often America's professed ideals are used as political maneuvers to cover up greed and corruption. Particularly problematic to María was the concept of Manifest Destiny. María wrote, "I love California dearly. . . . I feel . . . strong hatred and contempt (like a good Mexican) for that 'Manifest Destiny.' . . . Of all the evil phrases ever invented . . . there is not one phrase more detestable for me. . . . When I hear it, and I see as if in a photographic instance, all that the Yankies have done to make Mexicans suffer. . . . If I could believe in 'Manifest Destiny,' I would stop believing in justice or divine wisdom."[15] Though the book was hardly a huge success, it did receive some praise from critics and produced modest profits for the author.

After the death of her husband, María returned to Rancho Jamul and attempted to rebuild her life. She found great challenges waiting for her, as the title to the land was undefined, since her husband died without leaving a will. Determined not to lose the land, María would spend the next twenty-three years fighting legal battles. She hired attorneys and drew on her husband's political connections for assistance. To pay legal bills, she mortgaged the land, but the bank claimed she lacked the right to mortgage the property and brought a lawsuit against her in an effort to acquire the estate.

María's experience was far from isolated—in fact, it was part of a larger movement to pry land from Mexican ownership, though the Treaty of Guadalupe Hidalgo promised that Mexican land grants established prior to the war would be honored. The treaty read: "In the said territories, property of every kind, now belonging to Mexicans now established there, shall be inviolably respected. The present owners, the heirs of these, and all Mexicans who may hereafter acquire said property by contract, shall enjoy with respect to it guarantees equally ample as if the same belonged to citizens of the United States."[16]

Unfortunately, the treaty was not upheld. White squatters encroached on Mexican property, oftentimes erecting extensive building and cultivation projects. The laws favored the squatters and actually forced the owners of the land to pay taxes both on the squatters' improvements and profits! Many of the Mexican owners, including María, had few liquid assets—land was their main resource. Squatters and complicit officials attempted to embroil these landowners in costly legal battles they couldn't afford. When legal bills piled up, the owners inevitably had to sell their land or mortgage it. Further complicating the process was the fact that many original documents were in Spanish while the courts operated in English; Spanish-speaking landowners remained dependent on lawyers and judges to fairly translate court proceedings, which they often failed to do. Owners were frequently charged outrageous rates for the translation of documents, and court cases took years to process, during which the squatters built houses and cultivated land to increase the financial burden on the owners. One contemporary lawyer, representing a *Californio* client, wrote of the land commission, "I have no further confidence in this Board & I am fully satisfied that they are—or at least 2 of them are—Squatters, and were appointed by squatters."[17]

In spite of the time spent fighting legal battles, María and her children worked to improve the ranch, running cattle, growing wheat, barley, and castor beans. Hillsides covered in wildflowers supported productive beehives. María worked on an irrigation project to supply San Diego with water and started a cement company with lime produced on the ranch. She traveled to Washington, where she lobbied Congress to pass a special act to help the *Californio* cause. When one lawyer abruptly dropped her case, María wrote the entire legal brief herself, which was deemed forceful and articulate.

As an outlet for her continued frustration over the conflict, María began writing her second novel, *The Squatter and the Don.* Published in 1885, it is the first novel written in English about the land dispute from the Mexican perspective. Though the book is frequently classified as historical romance, it has drawn comparisons to *Uncle Tom's Cabin,* another book that uses the historical romantic novel to engage the reader in a message of social protest. The subtitle of María's book was *A Novel Descriptive of Contemporary Occurrences in California*. She published the novel under the pseudonym C. Loyal, which stands for *Ciudadano Leal* or "loyal citizen," a standard phrase for closing official documents in Mexico.

The novel recounts the story of a Spanish don who owns a 47,000-acre cattle ranch granted before the Mexican-American war; his ranch has been invaded by squatters who have built homes the don is forbidden to remove. The son of one of the squatters falls madly in love with the daughter of the don, in a Romeo-and-Juliet-style romance. Though the romance is a bit sensationalized and maudlin for modern readers, contemporary scholars have suggested that many female novelists of the eighteenth century used the romance novel as a socially acceptable way to write about political issues. Ethical and kind even when it leaves him open to exploitation, the don muses, "I think but few Americans know or believe to what extent we have been wronged by congressional action."[18] Discrimination against the Mexican inhabitants is a prominent theme of the novel. One character suggests dealing with the "greasers" by shooting them "as we shoot their cattle." The corrupt Gasbag responds, "O, no. No such violent means are necessary. All we have to do is to take their lands, and finish their cattle."[19]

The romance is happily resolved and the lovers marry, but by the end, the novel form drops away entirely and plot disappears into a political manifesto against unchecked capitalism and materialism. The even-handed don recognizes that systems beyond the squatters are at fault and says, "I don't blame the squatters; they are at times like ourselves, victims of a wrong legislation, which unintentionally cuts both ways. They were set loose upon us, but a law without equity recoils upon them more cruelly. Then we are all sufferers, all victims of a defective legislation and subverted moral principles."[20]

By the end of the novel, it is clear that all inhabitants of the United States, regardless of ethnicity, suffer as a result of unbridled greed and corruption.

As María focused on ranch projects, lawsuits, and writing, her children started families of their own. Nellie married and settled in San Diego, while Henry remained with his wife on the ranch, helping his mother with the maintenance. By this time, the land had been significantly reduced by 160 different squatters who claimed various portions. María traveled frequently for business, seeking different ways to address the land disputes. On one of these trips to Chicago, she passed away at the age of sixty-three from gastric fever. Her body was returned to San Diego for a large funeral, and she was laid to rest in the Calvary Catholic Cemetery.

María's novels were out of print for more than one hundred years, but in the 1990s, a revitalized interest in Mexican-American literature led to the reprinting of both of her novels in an ongoing effort to discover previously silenced Hispanic voices. Viewed as important recovered texts, scholarly attention has focused on María Ruiz de Burton as the first female Mexican-American author to write in English and one of the earliest contributors to Chicana literature, which is defined as literature by writers of Hispano-American origins, with concepts of culture and identity at the heart of their work.

María remained both involved in U.S. society and apart from it; her privileged position allowed her access to elite circles, but her identity as a Mexican and as a woman made her continuously aware of her separateness. She wrote, "Remember that I am a woman . . . and Mexican . . . with my soul enclosed in an iron cage. In this manner Society confines us as soon as we are born, like the Chinese and the feet of their women."[21] Her work contains contradictions, and critics note her disdain for lower socioeconomic classes. Familiar with both the roles of conqueror as well as conquered, she was both above and below, within and without—straddling borders of many kinds.

María's life, in addition to containing a fascinating and under-appreciated aspect of the American West, provides a broader context for analyzing current power structures embedded in public conversations that continue today. Certainly her life illuminates the complexity of current immigration issues with Latin America. Her insight on the irony of the overall rejection of Mexican language, culture, and immigrants in the United States, combined with a willingness to simultaneously profit off the vast resources that resulted from the conquest of Mexican lands, remains compelling and relevant. In a number of ways, it seems that many of us in the U.S. still try to discuss the issues of immigration without acknowledging its complicated origins.

María's life reminds me that history forces us to ask hard questions. Her story invites us to face our own assumptions and confront our own prejudices. In the words of María's Don, "The conquered always have but a weak voice, which nobody hears."[22] In the act of writing, and through her works' later rediscovery, María Ruiz de Burton successfully transcends two main effects of oppression: invisibility and the silencing of certain voices. We are reminded that we can listen with empathy and compassion to those who suffer injustice. We can also use our power, where we have it, to alleviate suffering in all of its forms.

FURTHER READING

Conflicts of Interest: The Letters of María Amparo Ruiz de Burton, edited, with commentary, by Rosaura Sánchez and Beatrice Pita (Houston, TX: Arte Público Press, 2001).

Amelia María de la Luz Montes and Anne Elizabeth Goldman, eds., *María Amparo Ruiz de Burton: Critical and Pedagogical Perspectives* (Lincoln: University of Nebraska Press, 2004).

Susan Cummins Miller, ed., *A Sweet, Separate Intimacy: Women Writers of the American Frontier, 1800–1922* (Salt Lake City: University of Utah Press, 2000).

María Amparo Ruiz de Burton, *The Squatter and the Don* (Houston, TX: Arte Público Press, 1992).

NOTES

1. Joyce W. Warren and Margaret Dickie, eds., *Challenging Boundaries: Gender and Periodization* (Athens: University of Georgia Press, 2000), 212.
2. Accessed at https://www.archives.gov/education/lessons/guadalupe-hidalgo.
3. Accessed at http://www.sandiegohistory.org/journal/84summer/burton.htm.
4. Ibid.
5. Warren and Dickie, *Challenging Boundaries,* 214.
6. *Conflicts of Interest: The Letters of María Amparo Ruiz de Burton*, edited, with commentary, by Rosaura Sánchez and Beatrice Pita (Houston, TX: Arte Público Press, 2001), 11.
7. Vicki L. Ruiz and Virginia Sánchez Korrol, eds., *Latina Legacies: Identity, Biography, and Community* (New York: Oxford University Press, 2005), 72.
8. *Conflicts of Interest*, 72.
9. Letter to Mariano Vallejo, in ibid.
10. Some sources conflict regarding the timing of the writing of this play. The chronology of writing it in San Diego and later publication is confirmed by Rosaura Sanchez and Beatrice Pita in their chapter "María Amparo Ruiz de Burton and the Power of her Pen," in Ruiz and Korrol, *Latina Legacies,* 74.
11. Amelia María de la Luz Montes and Anne Elizabeth Goldman, eds., *María Amparo Ruiz de Burton: Critical and Pedagogical Perspectives* (Lincoln: University of Nebraska Press, 2004), 215.
12. March 8, 1860. Accessed at http://www.sandiegohistory.org/journal/84summer/burton.htm.
13. De la Luz Montes and Goldman, *María Amparo Ruiz de Burton*, 247.
14. The novel was published anonymously, but it was filed with the Library of Congress under the names H. S. Burton and Mrs. Henry S. Burton.
15. Letter from María Amparo Ruiz de Burton to M. G. Vallejo, Feb. 15, 1869, in de la Luz Montes and Goldman, *María Amparo Ruiz de Burton,* 250.
16. The Treaty of Guadalupe Hidalgo, Article VIII, in de la Luz Montes and Goldman, *María Amparo Ruiz de Burton,* 253.
17. Warren and Dickie, *Challenging Boundaries,* 220.
18. María Amparo Ruiz de Burton, *The Squatter and the Don* (Houston: Arte Público Press, 1992), 17.
19. Ibid., 24.
20. Ibid., 28.
21. "Staten Island," August 12, 1869, in María Amparo Ruiz de Burton, *Who Would Have Thought It?* Edited with an Introduction and Notes by Amelia María de la Luz Montes (New York: Penguin Books, 2009).
22. Ruiz de Burton, *The Squatter and the Don,* 17.

CHAPTER 5

LUZENA STANLEY WILSON
FRONTIER ENTREPRENEUR

Born: May 1, 1819, North Carolina
Died: July 11, 1902, San Francisco, California

"The rags and tatters of my first days in California are well nigh forgotten in the ease and plenty of the present. The years have been full of hardships, but they have brought me many friends."[1]

When gold rush fever came to the prairies of Missouri in 1849, Mason Wilson caught the bug. He couldn't leave quickly enough, and he told his wife that he would get to California, make a fortune, then send for her and their children. But Luzena wouldn't hear of such a proposal. She later recalled, "I would not be left behind. I thought where he could go I could, and where I went I could take my two little toddling babies. . . . I little realized then the task I had undertaken. If I had, I think I should still be in my log cabin in Missouri."[2]

The couple spent a handful of days preparing a wagon with bedding, clothing, and food supplies before setting off on the two-thousand-mile journey to California without bothering to sell their land. Based on reports and rumors, the thought of encountering Native Americans terrified Luzena; but in spite of the accounts, her initial meeting with Native Americans proved uneventful. Still nervous, however, Luzena begged to join the first group of settlers they encountered, thinking their company would offer additional protection. The all-male Independence Company refused the Wilsons' companionship, saying they didn't want to be burdened with a woman and children on their way to California. Luzena wrote, "My anger at their insulting answer roused my courage, and my last fear of Indians died a sudden death."[3] The fast-moving company soon disappeared in the distance, but they left behind a woman even more determined to succeed.

Like most pioneers, Luzena found the journey to be more difficult than anticipated. Recounting the journey years later to her daughter, she wrote, "Nothing but actual experience will give one an idea of the plodding, unvarying monotony, the vexations, the exhaustive energy, the throbs of hope, the depths of despair, through which we lived."[4] The travelers soon tired of unvarying and scanty food, frequently broken wagons, and dangerous river crossings. Luzena recalled hastily dug graves and men who abandoned their wagons to return home.

The Wilsons discarded pots and pans and other superfluous items early in the journey, but, faced with the difficulty of mountain passages, Mason insisted they needed to remove more. Looking over their supplies, Luzena declared the only items they could do without were three slabs of bacon and a dirty calico apron, which they laid by the roadside. While her husband repaired the wagon, Luzena washed the apron and rendered the fat out of the bacon, sliced it, and reloaded the items without telling Mason. The next day he remarked several times that the oxen were doing much better and it was a very good thing they had left the "discarded" items behind.

During one of the most difficult sections of the trail, the Wilsons came upon the same group that initially refused their company. Many of the group had died; others had returned to Missouri. The few that remained were dying of hunger. Luzena didn't hold a grudge against the men and brought the sufferers food and water. She certainly didn't need to say "I told you so," since the grateful men fell on their knees and begged her forgiveness for refusing her presence. The California Trail proved a surmountable challenge for any person, male or female. That Luzena survived it with a baby and small toddler demonstrates the extent of this woman's strength and tenacity.

Among the earliest gold rushers, Luzena encountered few other women along the trail, a fact that brought her a certain amount of notoriety and respect. She realized how powerful this notoriety could be as they made camp for the last night, and she prepared a simple supper over the campfire. When she pulled a pan of biscuits from the heat, a hungry miner approached and said, "I'll give you five dollars, ma'am, for them biscuit."[5] The amount sounded like a fortune to Luzena, and she looked at him in surprise. Seeing her hesitation, he quickly countered that he would "give ten dollars for bread made by a woman" and laid a piece of gold in her hand. Marveling at the good fortune (ten dollars then would be more than three hundred dollars in today's currency), she handed over the biscuits and started making another pan for her family. In that moment Luzena discovered that there was more than one way to strike gold in the mining towns of the West.

Arriving in Sacramento, Luzena found a "city" comprised of three or four wooden buildings and hundreds of canvas tents and campfires. The Wilsons sold their oxen and used the proceeds to buy two rooms which they operated as a hotel. The inhabitants marveled at Luzena "as at a strange creature" and passed around her babies as a novelty.[6] In the first six months they spent in Sacramento, Luzena recalled seeing only two other women. In a town filled with a lot of homesick men, the arrival of mail by stagecoach provided the highlight of each day. Food items and imported goods sold for outrageous prices, and coins were scarce, so gold dust served as currency—one pinch equaled a dollar. More immigrants poured daily into the city, arriving by both wagon and ship.

Luzena's main memory of the following years was one of endless work. "We did things that our high-toned servants would now look at aghast, and say it was impossible for a woman to do. . . . It was a hand to hand fight with starvation at the first." Whatever needed to be done, Luzena found a way to do it.

After a few months, the Wilsons sold their interest in the hotel and invested the profits in barley. The couple had a thousand dollars of the grain waiting to go to market when it started to rain. Unfortunately, the rain didn't stop. For days, the downpour continued until the streets ran with water. One afternoon, the town crier galloped through town with the disastrous news: "the levee's broke!"[7] and all available men rushed to raise sandbags.

Meanwhile, Luzena was at home cooking dinner with her children when small rivulets of water began trickling over the ground. Soon the water rushed across the floor of her house. She snatched up her children and placed them on the bed, then packed up clothes and valuables. After carrying her children to the hotel across the street, she returned to grab bedding and the dinner she had been cooking. By the time she reentered the house, water six inches high streamed across the floor, and when she made her way back to the hotel, water surged around her knees, nearly knocking her over with its force. Others joined Luzena in the hotel, where they watched the water continue to rise as boat owners navigated the flood, rescuing the stranded and sodden.

The deluge forced evacuees to higher and higher floors of the hotel, until at last they huddled on the top floor, terrified the entire building would be swept away. Trapped with forty people in a large storeroom for seventeen days, hanging blankets provided the only two women with a scant measure of privacy. For food, they "caught the sacks of onions or boxes of anything which went floating by" or took a rowboat out to look for provisions.[8] To pass the time, the captives told stories, sang, and played cards. For the rest of Luzena's life, she could not hear the sound of relentless rain without "creeping over me the dread of the rising waters."[9]

When the waters finally subsided, settlers emerged from the hotel to an unrecognizable town covered with decaying animal carcasses, slime, and sediment. Remarkably, the Wilsons found their rusty stove and tent canvas, which they used to build a shelter. The barley harvest had been washed away, and the family was once again penniless. Afraid the floodwaters might return, the Wilsons decided to start over in Nevada City, where gold had recently been discovered. The only problem was they lacked a way to get there.

Ever-resourceful, Luzena managed to find a teamster willing to take her family, stove, and two sacks of flour to Nevada City for seven hundred dollars. Though she had no money, she promised to pay the driver back and "go security for the money,"[10] so they started on the difficult journey of sixty miles that lasted twelve long days due to horrific road conditions. They arrived in Nevada City completely covered in mud, and Luzena recalled that she had to scrub the children until her arms ached before returning "the children back to their natural hue."[11]

Lacking a tent, Mason built a hasty construction out of branches and left to find sturdier building materials. While he was gone, Luzena considered what she might do to help improve the family finances. Noticing a canvas tent with a sign that said: "Wamac's Hotel—Meals $1.00" across the way, she decided to start a competing business. She chopped stakes and drove them into the ground, then used some of the family's remaining funds to buy a few boards of lumber, which she set across the stakes for a table. Finally, she bought provisions and set about cooking a meal. "When my husband came back at night he found, mid the weird light of the pine torches, twenty miners eating at my table. Each man as he rose put a dollar in my hand and said I might count him as a permanent customer."[12] In six weeks, Luzena paid back the seven hundred dollars she had promised.

Luzena called her hotel El Dorado; soon the couple built a frame home and added on to it several times as business expanded. At the height of the hotel's popularity, Luzena hosted 75 to 200 boarders a week, and she soon hired a cook and waiters to assist. Operating a bustling hotel on the frontier was never dull. One night, while sitting snuggly by the kitchen fire, Luzena heard the sound of knocking from all sides of the frame house. Picking up a candle, she discovered angry faces pressed up against each of the windows, while voices shouted, "Burn the house!"[13] Terrified, she cracked open the door to find an angry mob congregating on her property. The sheriff explained that a murder had been committed by one of Luzena's boarders at a gambling hall; now the dead man's friends wanted revenge. Shaking with fear, Luzena let the men search her house, though the search proved fruitless. The next day, Luzena learned that the murderer had been in the crowd all along, disguised as a member of the mob.

Rough-and-tumble Nevada City sprang up overnight as highly productive mines poured money into the town. The Wilsons soon added a profitable store to their real estate holdings. Even the digging of a well frequently brought about a new discovery of gold. The town lacked a bank, however, so many of Luzena's boarders trusted her with their gold diggings. She stored them in her oven and underneath her bed in bags and pans, at times going to sleep with two hundred thousand dollars hidden in the home. In her kitchen she hung a purse of silver coins earned from sewing. One day the purse went missing; after a search, she found her youngest son in the street, busy building houses with coins in the dirt. Passersby smiled at the boy, but no one in the gold-rich town had touched the money.

On a night that began like any other, the Wilsons heard one of the most terrifying sounds ever heard in a frontier settlement. The clanging of bells and shouts of "Fire!" drove the Wilsons from their bed. The couple grabbed their clothes, children, a small amount of money, and fled for their lives. They joined the rest of the town's inhabitants in the streets to watch as the blaze spread from one wooden building to the next. Luzena described the moment: "We stood with bated breath, and watched the fiery monster crush in his great red jaws the homes we had toiled to build."[14] By dawn, the town lay in smoldering ruins. Eight thousand people became homeless, the Wilsons among them. Out of the tens of thousands of dollars they possessed when they went to sleep for the night, only five hundred remained by morning. Fortunately, a generous man allowed them to stay in his nearby cabin temporarily. In this borrowed bed, Luzena tossed and turned, ravaged with fever and discouragement.

She eventually rallied, as she always did, however, and once she was better, the Wilsons decided to return to Sacramento. Though they stayed only a few months, they found the town dramatically rebuilt since the flood. Buildings made from brick and stone had replaced the canvas tents, and sidewalks lined the streets. They set up house for a short time in a deserted hotel infested with rats, a problem that extended throughout the city. Even dogs and cats could do little to stop the growing pest population, and Luzena said, "[The rats] snapped at our heels as we passed. They bit at each other, and gnawed the legs of chairs where we sat. At night I put the bedding upon the tables, lest in our sleep the fierce creatures would be tempted to make their raids upon our bodies."[15]

After a few months of city life, the Wilsons found themselves longing for the beauty and solace of the country. They journeyed into the foothills, passing antelope and elk along the ridges. Coming upon a lovely valley named Vaca after its Spanish owner, the hills and wildflowers entreated them to stay, so they set up tent under the wide and reaching branches of a great old oak tree. Mason found work cutting hay, and once more, Luzena set up her stove. Making a table from the bed of the wagon, she printed "Wilson's Hotel" on a board with a piece of charcoal, and found herself in business.

For the whole summer, the family slept out of doors under the canvas wagon cover. Luzena said, "A row of nails driven close in the tree trunk held my array of culinary utensils and the polished tin cups which daily graced my table."[16] She loved the simplicity of their life and the ease of keeping house when there were no carpets or windows to be scrubbed. In the fall, the Wilsons constructed a frame house, though Luzena said at first it was difficult for her to sleep in the home as she had become so accustomed to sleeping in the open night air.

Spanish colonists and ranchers comprised most of the family's neighbors, and the Spanish adobe colony of Laguna Valley thrived nearby. They had been in the valley two months when Señor Vaca rode over to invite the family, with the help of an interpreter, to a ball at his house. In her diary, Luzena remarked on the "Mexican character of slothfulness," but admitted she knew very little of their customs. After she attended the ball at Señor Vaca's home, she wrote of the dazzling beauty of the adobe house lit by candles, and further commented on the guitar and tambourine music played for dancers who "fluttered their silken vari-colored scarfs, and bent their lithe bodies in graceful dances which charmed my cotillion and quadrille-accustomed eyes."[17] The brilliant colors of silk petticoats, and the men's velvet jackets decorated with gold braid also drew her praise. The food, served at midnight, included "savory Spanish stews, hot with chilies, great piles of tortillas, and gallons of only tolerable whisky."[18]

Luzena's nearest English-speaking neighbors were twelve miles away. After six months in the valley, she saddled her horse, packed a lunch, tied her boys behind her "with a stout rope,"[19] and set off for a visit. Lacking the benefit of a road, she headed in the general direction of the neighbor's house, which lay on the other side of herds of Spanish cattle. Luzena said the cattle, with their sharp, pointed horns, were "dangerous to encounter, even mounted, and to any one on foot they were certain death."[20] In the midst of this intimidating herd, a gust of wind blew the hat from her young son's head. Not wanting to lose the hat, but aware that she could not dismount without risking a stampede, Luzena knotted handkerchiefs together as a stirrup for her son to use as he quickly climbed down, snatched the hat, and returned to safety. The Wilsons paid their visit, and Luzena became good friends with the Wolfskills.

More neighbors arrived soon enough, however, bringing land disputes with them. The rudimentary practices used to initially determine property boundaries only compounded the problem. Spanish claims frequently disagreed with United States boundaries, and corrupt officials profited from the errors. Though the Wilsons' property lines were initially ruled to be valid, the decision was later reversed by a different commissioner. Meanwhile, a band of squatters took advantage of the Wilsons' brief absence to take up residence on part of the property, throwing up a hasty cabin in support of their claim.

When Mason returned, he set out in a fury to force the squatters from the property, but Luzena, afraid for his life, insisted he bring a witness in case the squatters turned violent. Fortunately, Mason found the men sleeping, their guns loaded and waiting. Mason and his friend took control of the weapons and forced the sleepy intruders from their beds. While his companion turned a gun on the angry men, Mason made quick work of destroying the cabin and lectured them to never again attempt the unlawful seizure of someone else's land. Though the squatters swore revenge, they disappeared without further complaint. However, the legal disputation over the property boundaries stretched into years and was such a frequent topic of conversation among their parents that the children would often "play at being 'squatters.'"[21]

As time passed, Luzena helped start a school for the neighborhood children and also gave birth to a daughter. When a physician paid his hotel bill with a medicine chest, she became a "general practitioner and apothecary for the neighborhood." Friends and acquaintances sought out her medical advice and counsel. She recalled, "I dealt out blue-mass, calomel, and quinine to patients from far and near; inspected tongues and felt pulses, until I grew so familiar with the business that I almost fancied myself a genuine doctor. I don't think I ever killed anybody."[22]

In front of the Wilsons' eyes, the frontier of Vaca Valley became Vacaville, a thriving agricultural center with flourishing vineyards. It must have been difficult for Luzena when, in 1872, Mason abruptly abandoned his family and departed for Texas. The reasons for his departure were never entirely clear, but some reports indicate he struggled with mental illness.[23] Luzena remained in Vacaville for five more years, but after another fire destroyed much of her property, she moved to San Francisco, supported by the profits of her real estate holdings.[24] When she took up residence in a hotel, she enjoyed being a guest rather than a host. Luzena's adult children lived busy and successful lives, inspired by their mother. Her oldest son graduated from Harvard Law School and daughter Correnah served on the board of Mills College.

In 1881, her beloved Correnah became quite ill. As Luzena cared for her sick daughter, she recounted the stories of their early days in California to pass the hours. In spite of her condition, Correnah wrote the stories down word for word as her mother recounted them,[25] and the women later published the resulting manuscript. Luzena concludes her memoir with these words: "The rags and tatters of my first days in California are well-nigh forgotten in the ease and plenty of the present. The years have been full of hardships, but they have brought me many friends."[26]

In many ways, Luzena's life represents the quintessential pioneer experience. She lived her life on geographical and metaphorical borders and edges, without any of the modern safety nets of insurance and fire departments. Her story illustrates the pros and cons of tossing these social structures into the road. On the one hand, the lack of structure left her free from considerations of business licenses and food handling permits. Improving her financial situation involved nothing more than sticking a sign on her wagon, producing good food, and turning a profit—overnight success didn't leave her owing large amounts of federal taxes, either. On the other hand, she could, and did, lose everything just as swiftly but as natural disasters devastated her homes time and time again, she didn't call for the government to declare a state of emergency. She didn't wait for a nonexistent insurance company to cut her a check. She started again with whatever she had—an iron kettle and a scrap of wood if that was all that remained.

Her stubbornness and grit is an impressive legacy. The fact that her children achieved education and success indicates that her tenacity became a family endowment. Scrappy Luzena did whatever needed to be done. If someone needed a teacher, she learned to teach; if they needed a doctor, she studied medicine. Although something is certainly gained in a world where people obtain credentials and certifications, something may be lost as well. Her inclination to learn what needed to be learned, figure out what needed figuring, and trust herself to gain the necessary skills and information to survive marks her as a true pioneer in every sense of the word. She refused to admit failure and doggedly endured in spite of relentless challenge. Luzena's life reminds me that I should probably complain about the trivial annoyances of my daily life less than I am apt to do—and I definitely should never let them stand in the way of building the life I want out of whatever materials happen to be at hand.

FURTHER READING

Christiane Fischer, *Let Them Speak for Themselves: Women in the American West 1849–1900* (New York: Shoestring Press, 1977).

Gloria G. Harris and Hannah S. Cohen, *Women Trailblazers of California: Pioneers to the Present* (Charleston, SC: History Press, 2012).

Fern Henry, *My Checkered Life: Luzena Stanley Wilson in Early California* (Nevada City, CA: Carl Mautz Publishing, 2003).

Brandon Marie Miller, *Women of the Frontier: 16 Tales of Trailblazing Homesteaders, Entrepreneurs, and Rabble-Rousers* (Illinois: Chicago Review Press, 2013).

Correnah Wilson Wright, *Luzena Stanley Wilson '49er: Her Memoirs as Taken Down by Her Daughter in 1881* (Oakland, CA: Eucalyptus Press, Mills College, 1937).

NOTES

1. Correnah Wilson Wright, *Luzena Stanley Wilson '49er: Her Memoirs as Taken Down by Her Daughter in 1881* (Oakland, CA: Eucalyptus Press, Mills College, 1937), 61.
2. Ibid., 2.
3. Ibid., 3.
4. Ibid.
5. Ibid., 9.
6. Other historians indicate that Luzena exaggerated the scarcity of women. They were scarce, but perhaps not as scarce as she liked to indicate. Still, her goods and services certainly received a generous reception.
7. Wright, *Luzena Stanley Wilson,* 20.
8. Fern Henry, *My Checkered Life: Luzena Stanley Wilson in Early California* (Nevada City, CA: Carl Mautz Publishing, 2003), 59.
9. Wright, *Luzena Stanley Wilson,* 22.
10. Ibid., 24.
11. Ibid., 27.
12. Ibid.
13. Ibid., 29.
14. Ibid., 35.
15. Ibid., 41.
16. Ibid., 46.
17. Ibid., 51.
18. Ibid.
19. Ibid., 47.
20. Ibid.
21. Ibid., 54.
22. Ibid., 57.
23. Henry, *My Checkered Life,* 148–49.
24. Gloria G. Harris and Hannah S. Cohen, *Women Trailblazers of California: Pioneers to the Present* (Charleston, SC: History Press, 2012), 20.
25. Some sources indicate that Correnah took word-for-word dictation, while others point out that Correnah was far more educated than her mother and the clean and lively prose probably contained a fair amount of editing. See Henry, *My Checkered Life,* 153, for a more in-depth discussion.
26. Wright, *Luzena Stanley Wilson,* 61.

CHAPTER 6

MOTHER JONES
SHE COULD NOT BE SILENCED

Born: May 1, 1837, Cork, Ireland
Died: November 30, 1930, Adelphi, Minnesota

"Coal miners have had no more staunch supporter, no more able defender than the one we all love to call Mother."[1]

Some individuals are so charismatic they refuse to stay within the pages of history but instead linger as enduring cultural icons. Today you can find Mother Jones's face printed on T-shirts, her pithy sayings circulated as Internet memes, and her name proudly carried by an independent news source. In the decades following her death, her disappointed enemies gradually realized that even beyond the grave, Mother Jones's voice could not be silenced. Separating the persona from the person does prove difficult, but perhaps that's part of the charm; in the words of one of her contemporaries, "The career of this unique old agitator reads like romance. There is no other that can be compared to it."[2]

America has been called an experiment in capitalism, and certainly the late 1800s epitomized this claim. The wildly popular rags-to-riches stories of Horatio Alger were embodied in the lives of tycoons such as Andrew Carnegie and John D. Rockefeller. Anyone who wants to work hard, these stories promised, can leave poverty and soar to unimaginable wealth in the land of opportunity, this place called America.

But there was a dark side to capitalism. As agricultural

livelihoods dwindled, people and immigrants streamed to cities where they worked the newly created factories of a rapidly industrializing world. The fortunes of the wealthy were no longer built upon unpaid slave labor of the pre-Civil War world, but anyone examining the conditions of the poor in overcrowded cities could draw correlations between the two systems. Either way, the laborer traded the work of his hands day and night for an allowance of food. Either way, the laborer remained helpless to escape the system. In the words of Mother Jones, one of the greatest social activists of all time: "As one looks on this brood of helpless human souls one could almost hear their voices cry out, 'Be still a moment, O you iron wheels of capitalistic greed, and let us hear each other's voices, and let us feel for a moment that this is not all of life.'"[3]

Mary Harris Jones was born in County Cork, Ireland, in 1837.[4] Though her notoriously unreliable autobiography claims she was the child of a long line of rabble-rousers, that is probably an exaggeration.[5] What is clear, however, is that due to an oppressive tenant farmer system in Ireland, Mary's Irish Catholic family struggled to subsist. They watched the early developments of the Irish Potato Famine in horror, as thousands of sick and starving refugees streamed to the towns. Around her tenth birthday, Mary's father and older brother left for America, where they saved enough money to send for the rest of the family in the 1850s.

The family settled in Toronto, where Mary attended school and her father labored on a railway construction crew. After graduation, she taught school for a time; then she moved to Chicago to work as a dressmaker and later to Tennessee, where she met and married George E. Jones, an iron molder and proud member of the Iron Molders' Union. Mary gave birth to four children within a handful of years, and enjoyed being a mother. During those happy years in Memphis, she must have imagined her life continuing on in a fairly predictable course, as no one could have foretold the events that lay just around the bend.

The hot, humid environs of Memphis are lovely by winter, but by summer, rising temperatures create unbearable conditions for most living creatures, with one notable exception: the mosquito. As mosquito activity increased each summer, so did the epidemic of the dreaded yellow fever, though at the time, no one considered the two to be connected. In the yellow fever outbreak of 1867, the poor areas of Memphis with the worst sanitation saw record levels of illness. Wealthy inhabitants fled to the countryside as the death toll rose every day. Early symptoms of the disease include fever, chills, severe stomach pain, and hemorrhaging. Within a few days, however, the skin develops a yellow hue and the patient produces a black vomit[6] that indicates the end is near. Twenty-five hundred cases of yellow fever developed in Memphis that summer.[7]

Living in one of the poor areas of town, and lacking money to flee the city, Mary cared for her children as one by one they grew ill and succumbed to the ravages of the disease. Her five- and four-year-old daughters, her two-year-old son, and her baby girl all suffered as Mary and her husband tried desperately to save them. At last, her husband also developed the fever and rapidly declined. Within two weeks, Mary's entire family lay dead. Left to bury her husband and four children, she later recalled, "I sat alone through nights of grief. . . . All day long, all night long, I heard the grating of the wheels of the death cart."[8]

It is impossible to comprehend what Mary endured those few short weeks. In what is probably a residual effect of trauma, she rarely spoke of the time afterwards, glossing over the event with a few short sentences in her memoir. After burying her loved ones with the help of the Iron Molders' union, Mary returned to the city of Chicago to work as a dressmaker once more. With a grief-stricken heart, she set up shop near Lake Michigan and crafted dresses for wealthy patrons, marveling at the world of contrast between the opulent lives of her customers and the poverty on the streets of the city. She wrote, "Often while sewing for the lords and barons who lived in magnificence on the Lake Shore Drive, I would look out of the plate glass windows and see the poor, shivering wretches, jobless and hungry, walking along the frozen lake front. . . . My employers seemed neither to notice nor to care."[9]

Four years after Mary's arrival in the city, tragedy struck again when the Great Chicago Fire burned roughly three-and-a-half square miles of the city. Bereft of her shop as well as her home, Mary found refuge in the lake itself as the city burned, then huddled in a church, one of 100,000 people left homeless by the fire. In a fire-scorched building, Mary first listened to the Knights of Labor, a peaceful organization dedicated to uplifting the rights of the workingman. The progressive organization welcomed blacks, women, and Irish Catholics, though Asians were excluded, along with doctors, lawyers, liquor manufacturers, and other "unproductive" members of society.[10]

Mary joined the Knights of Labor, devoting herself to a cause all the more meaningful given her father's struggle in Ireland and her husband's connection to his union; in the process, she discovered she had a powerful gift for public speaking. Creating a persona to aid the movement, she exaggerated her age, wore old-fashioned black dresses, and resorted to dramatic and drastic measures to gain the attention of the nation. She became "Mother Jones," and all workers everywhere became her children. Ironically, by adopting this persona, Jones freed herself from the expectations for women in her day. On behalf of the cause of labor, she was able to travel independently, use rough language, and voice her opinion on political matters in passionate tones, activities that didn't exactly align with recommended etiquette in the popular *Lady's Guide to Perfect Gentility.*[11]

But speak her mind she did. Mary's ability to inspire a crowd reached mythical proportions. John Brophy, a miner from Pennsylvania, recalled: "When she started to speak, she could carry an audience of miners with her every time. Her voice was low and pleasant, with great carrying power. She didn't become shrill when she got excited; instead her voice dropped in pitch and the intensity of it became something you could almost feel physically."[12]

Mary entered the fight for labor at a precarious time. The economic depression of 1873 was the worst the United States had ever faced to that point. Low-income jobs were not only difficult to come by, but they paid wages on which it was nearly impossible to survive. Children worked twelve- to fourteen-hour days in mine shafts and factories. Accidents that left workers maimed or dead occurred frequently. In spite of the horrific work conditions, collective bargaining and unions were seen as "un-American," and almost without exception, police and law officials protected the interests of the business owners.

As the depression continued, doubts about capitalism soared in the face of unemployment. Mother Jones believed the greatest problem facing the country was class warfare. She favored socialism over capitalism and wanted to see the power structures of the country broken down, coupled with the rise of the working class.[13] Her socialist leanings were quite common for the time, and writers such as Jack London, Upton Sinclair, and Helen Keller also supported these drastic economic changes.

Some of the most visible faces of the nation's suffering were the millions of children working in factories and textile mills. To further understand the plight of these children, Mother Jones masqueraded as a mill worker, accepting mill jobs in Tuscaloosa, Alabama. She wrote of the experience, "I was given work in the factory, and there I saw the most heart-rending spectacle in all my life. . . . Little girls and boys, barefooted, walked up and down between the endless rows of spindles, reaching thin little hands into the machinery to repair snapped threads. . . . Tiny babies of six years old with faces of sixty did an eight-hour shift for ten cents a day. If they fell asleep, cold water was dashed in their faces; and the voice of the manager yelled above the ceaseless racket and whir of the machines."[14]

Enraged by the conditions she witnessed in the mills, Mary assisted with a Philadelphia mill strike in which 16,000 children walked out, demanding a reduction in their workweek from sixty to fifty-five hours.[15] To increase public awareness, Mary led a children's march from Philadelphia to New York City. In spite of mosquitoes and oppressive heat, they paraded from town to town for three weeks, holding rallies and carrying signs that read: "We want time to go to school," and "55 hours or nothing."[16] The hundred children slept in Grover Cleveland's barn, bathed in the Delaware River, ate food provided by sympathetic farmers, and held rallies each evening. Addressing one of the crowds, Mother Jones said, "We will parade up and down Wall Street to show the millionaires the little emaciated [children] . . . who have earned their millions for them."[17] The group eventually ended up at President Theodore Roosevelt's summer home on Long Island, Sagamore Hill. Though the President refused to see them, the children's march of 1903 brought tremendous publicity to the issue of child labor decades before the federal ban.[18]

Along with factory jobs, underground shaft mining was surely among the most dangerous jobs in the early twentieth century. In 1913, Mother turned her attention to the Rockefeller-owned coal mines of Colorado. The miners complained of election fraud, brutal mine guards, and payment in the form of scrip redeemable only at overpriced company stores. "I hate violence," Mother Jones once declared with characteristic humor, "I favor drama."[19] Both drama and violence played out in the strike fields of Colorado. When ninety percent of miners walked off the job, guards retaliated by forcing families from their homes in winter conditions. The union set up a makeshift settlement of tents, soon inhabited by 1,200 families. Tensions escalated as both sides stockpiled weapons, and the mine guards installed searchlights and guns aimed at the camps to further infuriate workers.

Mother Jones camped beside the miners, offering moral support and rousing speeches. She led a parade of 1,500 children from the camp through the nearby towns to raise public support. As tensions increased, the coal company convinced the governor to call in the National Guard. Paid soldiers stood guard, and local sheriffs and state troops clearly operated on the company's behalf. Mother Jones decided it was time to garner the attention of the nation, so she traveled the country, giving speeches and raising money for the miners. The governor took advantage of Jones's absence, issuing an edict forbidding her return. Never one to worry about orders, Mother returned anyway and was placed under house arrest. Knowing the media would report her actions, Mother Jones escaped, was recaptured, and finally placed in a prison that had been declared unfit for human habitation. It was a media nightmare, and her incarceration incited waves of protest. Letters flooded the White House and miners around the country marched, demanding her freedom. If she had been looking for drama, she had certainly found it.

Unfortunately, violence was not far behind. The coal company brought in new laborers to break the strike, while the original workers continued to suffer in cold, miserable camps. After three months of incarceration, the state released Mother Jones, and she left at once to testify in Washington, D.C. With Jones out of the state, National Guard troops tore down miners' tents, tossing families into the road, including a woman who had just given birth to twins. On April 19, 1914, while the Greek mining families celebrated Orthodox Easter, gunfire broke out. To this day, no one is sure who started the shooting, but women and children sheltered in hastily dug pits beneath the tents. When darkness fell, troops entered the camp, looting, setting fires to tents, and shooting strike leaders. By daybreak, twenty miners and their family members lay dead, including women and children.[20]

The Ludlow Massacre, as the event came to be called, erupted in the news, as mass meetings and demonstrations took place around the nation. In spite of Mother Jones's testimony to a U.S. House Commission, the investigating committee exonerated the mine company's actions. Faced at last with death and starvation, the miners called off the fourteen-month strike and returned to the mines. Though the immediate goals of the effort had failed, Mother Jones, now seventy-seven, traveled the country, recounting the story of the Ludlow Massacre. The event dramatically changed public opinion about large corporations and the importance of unions.

And in a broader sense, the event succeeded, as it brought about sweeping changes in the practice of business management. The Rockefellers fired their top managers, replacing them with employees deeply aware of the importance of an industry's image. New management wisely determined it was easier to improve working conditions than fight with striking workers. Though Mother Jones eventually reconciled with the Rockefellers, miners around the country continued to idolize the fiery woman who suffered so much on their behalf. One worker wrote: "Coal miners have had no more staunch supporter, no more able defender than the one we all love to call Mother."[21]

Considering Mother Jones's radical stance on workers' rights, one might conclude she also favored women's suffrage, but Jones actually did not support the movement. Disgruntled by capitalism and corruption in U.S. politics, Mary viewed the fight for women's suffrage as the continuation of a broken system. She considered the fight for the vote to be a wealthy white woman's issue, one that served as a distraction from a much larger problem. She stated, "Politics is only the servant of industry. The plutocrats have organized their women. They keep them busy with suffrage and prohibition and charity."[22]

Undoubtably impacted by the loss of her family, Mary felt that a woman's biggest contribution remained the raising of her children. She saw working families as the building block of broader society, a unit that functioned best when fathers were paid a livable wage. She said, "I am not a suffragist nor do I believe in 'careers' for women, especially a 'career' in factory and mill where most working women have their 'careers.' A great responsibility rests upon woman—the training of the children. This is her most beautiful task."[23] Though her view largely ignored the question of unmarried women or women who found fulfillment in their work, Mary's stance is best understood in the context of her focus on class struggle. She loved to point out: "I have never had a vote, and I have raised hell all over this country! You don't need a vote to raise hell! You need convictions and a voice!"[24]

For more than fifty years, Mary traveled the country speaking on behalf of child workers, steelworkers, deported Mexican workers, and coal miners. She once declared to a judge, "My address is wherever there is a fight against oppression. . . . My address is like my shoes: it travels with me."[25] Her tireless work on behalf of the destitute earned her indebted friends and bitter enemies. Jailed multiple times, she continued demanding fair wages, safe working conditions, and reasonable working hours for the nation's most vulnerable. Called "the most dangerous woman in America,"[26] Mother used creative approaches to draw attention to her cause, encouraging women to take their babies to the mines, and block the way of strikebreakers with brooms and mops. She helped in silk-weaving mills and copper mines, in telegraph offices and breweries. Into her nineties, she continued fighting and organizing.

∞

Many objectives for which Mother Jones fought have now been achieved: children are in schools, not factories; worker compensation laws protect people harmed in their employment; and the forty-hour workweek has become standard in the United States.

But in a multitude of other ways, her fight continues. All who struggle to survive paycheck to paycheck are her children. Her fight continues in the lives of migrant workers who pick the country's vegetables, where small children still often labor beside their parents. It continues in the meat-packing industry, where recruiting practices and dangerous working conditions are reminiscent of a bygone era. It continues as we import luxury items produced in overseas sweatshops and factories whose practices would not be permissible on our own soil. It continues in the current debate over democratic socialism, a dispute that centers on questions of who is responsible to assist the working poor and how that is best accomplished.

Mother Jones's voice echoes down the years, asking what price we are willing to pay for imported luxuries, cheap clothing, and inexpensive food. Are we willing to pay with the suffering of others? I imagine Mother Jones would want any examination of her life to lead back to a discussion of these contemporary issues. After all, she famously said, "Pray for the dead, and fight like hell for the living."[27] Mother Jones invites us to fight against corruption and abuse at every level, reminding us that the world will only be as fair as we demand it to be. She was not afraid to raise her voice in dialogue with the most educated and influential people of her day, and neither should we be. Over the course of her ninety-three years, she saw progress that filled her with hope. "The producer, not the meek, shall inherit the earth," she said near the end. "Not today perhaps, nor tomorrow, but over the rim of the years my old eyes can see the coming of another day."[28]

FURTHER READING

Elliott J. Gorn, *Mother Jones: The Most Dangerous Woman in America* (New York: Hill and Wang, 2001).

Judith Pinkerton Josephson, *Mother Jones: Fierce Fighter for Workers' Rights* (Minneapolis, MN: Lerner Publications, 1996).

S. Michele Nix, ed., *Women at the Podium: Memorable Speeches in History* (New York: HarperCollins, 2000).

Karenna Gore Schiff, *Lighting the Way: Nine Women Who Changed Modern America* (New York: Hyperion, 2005).

NOTES

1. Elliott J. Gorn, *Mother Jones: The Most Dangerous Woman in America* (New York: Hill and Wang, 2001), 87.

2. Written by Eugene V. Debs, originally published in *The Appeal to Reason,* November 23, 1907; later reprinted in *Debs: His Life, Writing and Speeches* (N.p.: Phil Wagner, 1908).

3. "Mother Jones," *International Socialist Review,* March 1901.

4. Historians believe that Mary exaggerated her age in order to augment the "grandmotherly" persona. August 1, 1837, is the baptism date recorded in County Cork records and is viewed to be accurate (see Gorn, *Mother Jones,* 9).

5. Mary's autobiography is acknowledged by historians to be highly colored and skewed—it was primarily written to persuade others to join the labor cause and was not intended to be highly committed to facts. According to more reputable sources, the family probably left Ireland due to the developing potato famine rather than the father's political activities (see Gorn, *Mother Jones,* 15–19).

6. Karenna Gore Schiff, *Lighting the Way: Nine Women Who Changed Modern America* (New York: Hyperion, 2005), 6–7.

7. Gorn, *Mother Jones,* 39–40.

8. Mary Harris Jones, *Autobiography of Mother Jones* (Chicago: Charles H. Kerr, 1925), 1.

9. Ibid., 2.

10. Marquita R. Walker, *The Daily Grind: How Workers Navigate the Employment Relationship* (Lanham, MD: Lexington Books, 2014), 49.

11. A popular manners guide published in 1856 by Emily Thornwell; the full title is *The Lady's Guide to Perfect Gentility in Manners, Dress, and Conversation, in the Family, in Company, at the Piano Forte, the Table, in the Street, and in Gentlemen's Society. Also a Useful Instructor in Letter Writing, Toilet*

Preparations, Fancy Needlework, Millinery, Dressmaking, Care of Wardrobe, the Hair, Teeth, Hands, Lips, Complexion, etc. I must admit that just reading the title of that book gives me a headache.

12. Gorn, *Mother Jones*, 74.

13. Ibid., 46.

14. Jones, *Autobiography*, 70.

15. Gorn, *Mother Jones*, 131.

16. Schiff, *Lighting the Way,* 52.

17. Gorn, *Mother Jones*, 134.

18. Child labor diminished over time, at first through state legislation. The federal ban did not come until 1938 (see Gorn, *Mother Jones,* 138–40). The Child Labor Public Education Project also did not come until 1938 (see https://www.continuetolearn.uiowa.edu/laborctr/child_labor/about/us_history.html).

19. Gorn, *Mother Jones,* 199.

20. Schiff, *Lighting the Way,* 86–91.

21. Gorn, *Mother Jones,* 87.

22. Jones, *Autobiography,* 125.

23. Ibid., 147.

24. Ibid., 125.

25. S. Michele Nix, ed., *Women at the Podium: Memorable Speeches in History* (New York: HarperCollins, 2000), 124.

26. Schiff, *Lighting the Way,* 70.

27. Gorn, *Mother Jones,* 3.

28. Jones, *Autobiography,* 147.

CHAPTER 7

ZITKALA-SA
DAKOTA SIOUX RIGHTS ACTIVIST AND WRITER

Born: February 22, 1876, South Dakota
Died: January 26, 1938, Washington, D.C.

"The paleface has stolen our lands and driven us hither. Having defrauded us of our land, the paleface forced us away. . . . We were driven, my child, driven like a herd of buffalo."[1]

Between, among, and below the lines of pioneer narratives hovers the awareness that the land to which the newcomers flocked was not uninhabited. What previous generations called "manifest destiny" looks a great deal like genocide from the perspective of later generations. Admiration for the grit and survival of the pioneers is marred by the attitude of racial superiority with which they met first nation peoples. As whites pressed west in increasingly high numbers, treaties promising land to native communities were broken, rewritten, and broken again. A fierce debate developed over the role first inhabitants of the continent should play in the new nation. A slightly less well-known aspect of the pioneer experience is that immigration also flowed from west to east, as evidenced by the life of Zitkala-Sa.

Zitkala-Sa was born as Gertrude Simmons on the Pine Ridge Reservation in South Dakota in 1876 to a white father and a Yankton-Nakota Sioux mother. Arriving in the world the same year as the Battle of Little Bighorn, at her mother's knee she learned of the tribe's forced march, which occurred after elders traded thousands of acres of land in return for a promised reservation. During the difficult retreat to the reduced-size, less-prosperous land, Gertrude's older sister and uncle both died. Tate I Yohin Win (Reaches for the Wind) told her daughter, "The paleface has stolen our lands and driven us hither. Having defrauded us of our land, the paleface forced us away. . . . We were driven, my child, driven like a herd of buffalo."[2]

In spite of these challenges, Gertrude recalled a happy childhood; she spent days learning beadwork in the tepee of her mother and later wrote, "I was as free as the wind that blew my hair, and no less spirited than a bounding deer."[3] She loved evening gatherings when storytellers recounted tribal legends by the light of a fire. Missionaries often visited the reservation, recruiting children for boarding schools in the East, and Gertrude's brother left to receive an education. When Gertrude was eight, the missionaries invited her to return with them. Speaking through a translator, they promised: "Yes, little girl, the nice red apples are for those who pick them; and you will have a ride on the iron horse if you go with these good people."[4]

Lured by promises of train rides and apples, Gertrude begged to go, but her mother was distraught at the thought of her daughter leaving. Tate said, "Though she does not understand what it all means, she is anxious to go. She will need an education when she is grown, for then there will be fewer real Dakotas, and many more palefaces. This tearing her away, so young, from her mother is necessary, if I would have her an educated woman . . . but I know my daughter must suffer keenly in this experiment."[5] At last convinced by Gertrude's aunt and the girl's own desire, Tate relented. Unfortunately, her mother's words proved prophetic: not only would the ensuing experience leave Gertrude painfully caught between two worlds, it would also cause an unresolvable rift between mother and daughter.

Gertrude received the promised train ride, and she arrived at the

Quaker-run White's Manual Labor Institute in Wabash, Indiana, an institution based on the philosophy of Captain Richard H. Pratt: "Kill the Indian and save the man." After stripping Gertrude of her traditional clothing, staff forbade the use of her native language, though she spoke no English at the time. In the Sioux tradition, braids were cut only by enemies as an act of war, but the teachers informed Gertrude that her hair would be cut. Terrified, Gertrude hid under the bed, only to be dragged from her hiding place and strapped down in a chair. "I cried aloud, shaking my head all the while until I felt the cold blades of the scissors against my neck, and heard them gnaw off one of my thick braids."[6] Traditional beliefs in the Great Spirit were repudiated while students were required to convert to Christianity. Gertrude would later claim the rigors of the school "bound my individuality like a mummy for burial."[7]

Though mourning the loss of tribe and family, Gertrude learned English quickly and devoured books. Even while she resented the harsh rigor of the school, her adept mind thirsted for the knowledge it provided. Three years passed before she returned to her mother, and when she did, Gertrude drifted about the reservation, feeling isolated and confused. No longer at home on the prairies she had idealized while away, the teen realized the true price she paid for education was a loss of belonging to either world. "Even nature seemed to have no place for me. I was neither a wee girl nor a tall one; neither a wild Indian nor a tame one."[8] She remained home for four years but decided, against her mother's wishes, to return to White's Institute when she was fifteen to continue her studies.

By the time she graduated four years later, Gertrude had become a skilled singer, orator, pianist, violist, and writer. When a music teacher left the school, Gertrude assumed her classes. At nineteen years of age, she delivered a graduation speech on the topic of women's suffrage. "Half of humanity cannot rise while the other half is in subjugation," she declared.[9] The *Wabash Times* called her speech "a masterpiece that has never been surpassed in eloquence or literary perfection by any girl in this county."[10] The performance so impressed a member of the audience, a wealthy woman who offered to pay for Gertrude to attend Earlham College. Though her mother again opposed the decision, Gertrude enrolled.

Pained by the rejection from her family, yet not fully accepted by her white peers, Gertrude found college an isolating experience. To overcome loneliness, she entered an oratorical contest, delivering to her entirely white audience an impassioned speech about Native American rights. "Unfortunately, civilization is not an unmixed blessing," she told them. "Broken treaties shake [the Indian's] faith in the newcomers. . . . He loved his native land. Do you wonder still that he skulked in forest gloom to avenge the desolation of his home? Is patriotism a virtue found only in Saxon hearts?"[11] She ended with a point that had been drummed into her consciousness in boarding school: the best hope for the native was to assimilate the white man's ways: "We seek to stand side by side with you. . . . Thy people shall be my people, and thy God my God." Her speech received enthusiastic applause, and she won first place in the contest.

A month later, she received an invitation to represent the college in another speech competition—she would be the only female presenter and the only Native American. Her classmates cheered when Gertrude arose to speak, but students from another college chose that moment to unfurl a flag decorated with a crude image of an Indian girl and the word "squaw" scrawled below. In spite of the painful display, Gertrude delivered her speech without faltering. When the winners were announced, the flag finally dropped out of sight. Gertrude won second place in the competition and returned to celebrations in her honor at Earlham.

A few months before graduation, Gertrude contracted an illness that left her unable to continue her studies. Instead, she took a teaching position at Carlisle, the most well-known Indian boarding school in the United States. Her employer was none other than Richard H. Pratt, the man known for his skill in training successful Indians by eradicating their culture. After a month of teaching, Gertrude was sent to the Yankton Reservation to recruit more students; in an ironic twist, she now enlisted new students for the painful experience she herself had undergone.

Gertrude had not been home in six years, and she found her family living in poverty. Reservation land had been encroached upon by white settlers since the Dawes Act allowed the sale of tribal land to white settlers.[12] Buffalo and other game had been hunted to near-extinction, and most Native Americans had become desperately poor, dependent on government food and goods. Since government agents forced native residents to farm the land, tribal members now lived too far away from each other to gather in the evenings.

Appalled by the disappearance of her childhood world, Gertrude returned to teach at Carlisle. She played in violin performances and sat for a session with a well-known photographer, but she grew increasingly aware of the sacrifices she had made to be successful. Burning with anger at the destruction of her culture and religion, she finally resigned her teaching post and went to Boston to study at the New England Conservatory of Music. With each passing year, she grew more certain that Indian culture was not inferior to white culture; in fact, in many ways she believed it was superior. Eventually, accumulated years of anger and injustice burst forth through her pen. Using the language that had been forced upon her, she wrote a series of articles for *The Atlantic Monthly*, adopting the name of Zitkala-Sa, Lakota for "Red Bird." She wrote: "I hate this eternal tug-of-war between being wild or becoming civilized. The transition is an endless evolution—that keeps me in continual Purgatory."[13]

The Protestantism that had been forced upon Zitkala-Sa in boarding school gave way to her conversion to Catholicism and finally a return to the deep connection with nature and the Great Spirit she had felt in her youth. She wrote a defense of these traditional ways: "A wee child toddling in a wonder world, I prefer to their dogma my excursions into the natural gardens where the voice of the Great Spirit is heard in the twittering of birds, the rippling of mighty waters, and the sweet breathing of flowers. If this is Paganism, then at present, at least, I am a pagan."[14]

Some critics praised her bravery for writing about her experience; others criticized her portrayal of negative incidents, while leaving out the "happier side of her school days."[15] Inspired by her publication success and cultural rediscovery, she collected tales from her childhood in a book called *Old Indian Legends,* a fairly controversial move on both sides. Since the stories were traditionally shared orally, many Native Americans felt that printing them in a single form in English disrespected the oral storytelling tradition, but Zitkala-Sa believed white society would never respect a culture about which they knew nothing. She wrote, "The old legends of America belong quite as much to the blue-eyed little patriot as to the black-haired aborigine. I have tried to transplant the native spirit of these tales— roots and all—into the English language, since America in the last few centuries has acquired a second tongue."[16]

Her cultural awakening impacted Zitkala-Sa's romantic life as well. Carlos Montezuma was a Yavapai doctor who hoped to marry her. Though she cared for him, Carlos sided with Pratt's ideas of adopting the white ways in order to be successful, while Zitkala-Sa now rejected this philosophy. Determined to reclaim her Yankton Sioux identity, she wrote: "While the old people last, I want to get from them their treasured ideas of life. This I can do by living among them."[17] She broke off her engagement to Carlos and married Raymond Bonnin instead, a Yankton from her reservation who had returned from boarding school to work for the Indian Service. Raymond helped Zitkala-Sa reconnect with her family, language, and culture, bringing her a measure of peace. A few years later when Raymond was offered a job on the Uintah Reservation in Utah, the couple relocated there.

In Utah, Zitkala-Sa found a continuation of the story she had witnessed in South Dakota. Ute Indians had been stripped of fruitful land,[18] reservation holdings had been reduced in size, and the game population had been decimated, leaving the Utes impoverished and dependent on the government. Tribal members were forbidden to leave the reservation, while white teachers enforced cultural eradication in schools. Zitkala-Sa began teaching in the Uintah Reservation school as the only Native American teacher, and she gave birth to a son named Ohiya. Though she enjoyed living among the Utes, as time passed she found herself longing for the music and culture of the East. When William Hanson, a high school music teacher in Utah, asked for Zitkala-Sa's help creating an opera based on Indian culture, she enthusiastically embraced the idea.

Zitkala-Sa suggested the opera should focus on the Plains Indians' Sun Dance, a ceremony that had been banned in 1883 as a "heathen rite."[19] Gertrude worked closely with Hanson for months on the project, playing traditional chants on her violin, ensuring the accuracy of the lyrics, and facilitating the involvement of tribal elders to determine which aspects of the sacred ceremony could be ethically presented to white audiences. *The Sun Dance Opera* was first performed by tribal members, high school students, and other residents in February 1913. Deemed "an artistic triumph," the twenty-four performances in Utah received attention from the national press.[20]

Revitalized by the success of the opera, the Bonnins moved to

Washington, D.C., where Raymond studied law and served in the army and Zitkala-Sa resumed writing and lecturing on behalf of Native American rights. Zitkala-Sa joined the Society of American Indians (SAI) as the first female board member, lobbying Congress on behalf of Indian causes and contributing articles to the Society's magazine, which she eventually ran as editor-in-chief. Her voice became instrumental in fighting for Indian citizenship and suffrage, claiming that native peoples would continue to be abused by a government in which they had no voice.

After a brilliant speech to one of the most prestigious women's organizations in the country, the Indian Welfare Committee hired Zitkala-Sa to investigate the federal government's treatment of Native Americans in Oklahoma. She traveled with an attorney and a member of the IRA to scrutinize claims of land theft. The team unearthed horrific stories of extortion, rape, abuse, and even murder of Native Americans in order to acquire property. In one of many such stories, a seven-year-old Choctaw girl inherited twenty acres of land, but the court-appointed white guardian paid the girl and her grandmother a living allowance so small it left them on the point of starvation. Sick and emaciated, the girl was removed to an Indian school for her protection, but her white guardian appeared and demanded her return. A month later, the girl was dead, her property now in the possession of her court-assigned protector. Story after story such as this one surfaced, as evidence demonstrated that guardians, courts, and lawyers had appropriated up to seventy percent of Indian estates in return for their "guardianship."[21]

The resulting thirty-nine-page report, "*Oklahoma's Poor Rich Indians: An Orgy of Graft and Exploitation of the Five Civilized Tribes, Legalized Robbery,*" caused an explosion of controversy, eventually prompting congressional investigation. Though the subcommittee exonerated the courts, the report proved instrumental in the 1934 adoption of the Indian Reorganization Act that returned the management of lands to tribes. Disgusted by the continued eradication of her people, Zitkala-Sa pointed out that only the methods of abuse had changed. She wrote, "To take the life of a nation during the slow march of centuries seems not a lighter crime than to crush it instantly with one fatal blow."[22] In 1926, she started the National Council of American Indians to continue fighting for greater equality.

Though she accomplished many important goals, others—like suffrage for all Native American people—remained elusive.[23] Impoverished and increasingly ill near the end of her life, Zitkala-Sa died on January 26, 1938, at the age of sixty-one. In spite of the close relationship she had with her husband, son, and four grandchildren, she died disillusioned and discouraged, torn by the loyalty she felt for her tribe and her inability to be satisfied by reservation life. She was haunted by the conflict that had never been fully resolved with her mother and angered by disagreements with other Indian activists about the best way to improve the lives of native peoples.

Four months after her death, the New York City Light Opera Guild brought Zitkala-Sa's *The Sun Dance Opera* to a Broadway stage. Two hundred soloists auditioned for leading roles, and the cast of singers and dancers was gathered from the Cherokee, Chippewa, Hopi, Mohawk, and Yakima nations. The show sold out 3,100 seats for all performances, and applause interrupted the show each night at several points. On stage for the New York audience, Zitkala-Sa's childhood world was brought to life: the scent of burning sage, the tepees pitched by a mountain stream, the drums that pounded beneath a chorus of the legends of the elders. In the grand finale, dancers performed sacred vows to the Great Spirit. Though the audience did not hear the story as Zitkala-Sa first did, "under an open sky, nestling close to the earth,"[24] the performance became a symbol of her long-sought-for identity—a mingling of the cultured world of musical theater with the stories and traditions of the land that would always be her first home.

꧁꧂

The tug-of-war that Zitkala-Sa endured was uniquely born out of the times and culture in which she lived, and the intensity and pain of it echoes to this day. Certainly there are still many ways in which individuals find themselves pulled by competing loyalties. In the United States today, 6.9 million people identify with two or more races. Eighty million people (twenty-five percent of the population) are first- or second-generation immigrants. With this in mind, we can understand why there is both the longing for and idealization of home, coupled with a growing attachment to the new: a disconnection from both frequently becomes the result.

It's difficult to read Zitkala-Sa's work and not feel compassion for her struggle. As a highly intelligent person, her desire to stay connected with her own disappearing culture seemed irreconcilable with the allure of a society that fed her artistically and intellectually; the fact that the same society perpetuated crimes against her own people must have rendered a harsh contradiction. I admire her bold use of the very skills taught by her oppressors to fight for the halt of continued abuse.

Today, of the remaining 5.2 million American Indians and Alaskan natives, 29.2 percent live in poverty—a higher level than any other racial group. One bright spot is that history books now more fully acknowledge this horrific chapter of U.S. history.

A continuation of the debate that raged during Zitkala-Sa's life regarding what should be done to remedy the converging of two worlds remains much more difficult to answer. Sometimes the only response is to stand in grief, mourning the loss. Zitkala-Sa struggled to know how best to deal with the society that had dealt out such treatment—did she embrace it because it educated her? Or reject it because it severed her from her dwindling people? She vacillated between both in a tortured emotional journey. Feeling like she hadn't accomplished nearly enough, she died unaware of how influential her life truly was, how very remarkable her gifts and accomplishments. She is a reminder to speak your truth and tell your story. Your own identity is worth fighting for, and it can be manifested in a way that reflects your own beliefs.

Today, U.S. communities remain as diverse as they have ever been—at times we view this as a modern development, but a closer look at history reveals that in fact the diversity has always been present, though the specific cultural makeup has changed over time. Regardless of our background, we may hesitate to reach either way across that cultural divide—to speak with neighbors down the street from Syria or ask an acquaintance from Guatemala about his or her life. We may hold back, afraid we will say something wrong or find we have nothing in common. However, it seems to me that the most dangerous, divisive weapon humanity holds is an inclination to define a group of people as "other" and thereby justify treating them as less. That spirit of divisiveness is almost always the true culprit behind war and poverty and genocide, wielded by dictators and bullies alike.

Connection and understanding remain the greatest weapons we have to fight against prejudice. Though it may require leaving our comfort zone, Zitkala-Sa invites us to find the courage to reach out, seeking for understanding. As we come to truly know one another, we find that we have much more in common than we might imagine. From such a space, we can create a worldview that sees others as part of the whole and part of humanity—deeply connected to ourselves and worthy of respect.

FURTHER READING

Susan Cummins Miller, *A Sweet, Separate Intimacy: Women Writers of the American Frontier, 1800–1922* (Salt Lake City: University of Utah Press, 2000).

S. Michele Nix, ed., *Women at the Podium: Memorable Speeches in History* (New York: HarperCollins, 2000).

Nancy M. Peterson, "From the Heart of Chaos: Finding Zitkala-Sa," in James A. Crutchfield, ed., *The Way West: True Stories of the American Frontier* (New York: Tom Doherty Associates, 2006).

Doreen Rappaport, *The Flight of Red Bird: The Life of Zitkala-Sa* (New York: Dial Books, 1997).

Zitkala-Sa, *American Indian Stories* (Washington: Hayworth Publishing House, 1921).

NOTES

1. Susan Cummins Miller, *A Sweet, Separate Intimacy: Women Writers of the American Frontier, 1800–1922* (Salt Lake City: University of Utah Press, 2000), 388.
2. Ibid.
3. Ibid., 387.
4. Zitkala-Sa, "Impressions of an Indian childhood: The big red apples," accessed online at http://digital.library.upenn.edu/women/zitkala-sa/stories/stories.html.
5. Ibid.
6. Zitkala-Sa, "Impressions of an Indian childhood: The cutting of my long hair," accessed online at http://digital.library.upenn.edu/women/zitkala-sa/stories/stories.html.
7. Miller, *Sweet, Separate Intimacy,* 392.
8. Zitkala-Sa, "Impressions of an Indian childhood: Four strange summers," accessed online at http://digital.library.upenn.edu/women/zitkala-sa/stories/stories.html.
9. Doreen Rappaport, *The Flight of Red Bird: The Life of Zitkala-Sa* (New York: Dial Books, 1997), 58.
10. Ibid.
11. S. Michele Nix, ed., *Women at the Podium: Memorable Speeches in History* (New York: HarperCollins, 2000), 120.
12. An area of 138 million acres of Indian-owned land in the United States was reduced to 47 million acres because of the Act (see Rappaport, *Flight of Red Bird,* 77).
13. Rappaport, *Flight of Red Bird,* 13.
14. Zitkala-Sa, "Why I Am a Pagan," in Glynis Carr, ed., *The Online Archive of Nineteenth-Century U.S. Women's Writings,* accessed online at http://www.facstaff.bucknell.edu/gcarr/19cUSWW/ZS/WIAP.html.
15. Not surprisingly, her most vocal critic was Richard Henry Pratt, the director of the school that preached cultural eradication of native ways (see Rappaport, *Flight of Red Bird,* 85).
16. Zitkala-Sa, *Old Indian Legends* (Boston: Ginn, 1901), iv.
17. Rappaport, *Flight of Red Bird,* 88.
18. Two million acres were removed from reservation lands and given to nontribal members.

19. Nancy M. Peterson, "From the Heart of Chaos: Finding Zitkala-Sa," in James A. Crutchfield, ed., *The Way West: True Stories of the American Frontier* (New York: Tom Doherty Associates, 2006), 228.

20. Ibid.

21. R. David Edmunds, *The New Warriors: Native American Leaders Since 1900* (Lincoln: University of Nebraska Press, 2001), 48.

22. Nix, *Women at the Podium*, 122.

23. Though Congress passed the Indian Citizenship Act in 1924, giving Native Americans the possibility to vote, several laws and policies prohibited the exercise of that right. Utah was the last state to give Native Americans the right to vote in 1956.

23. Zitkala-Sa, *Old Indian Legends*, v.

CHAPTER 8

MARY HALLOCK FOOTE
MINING TOWN AUTHOR AND ILLUSTRATOR

Born: November 9, 1847, Milton, New York
Died: June 25, 1938, Boston, Massachusetts

One of Mary's illustrations: A Pretty Girl in the West

"The East constantly hears of the recklessness, the bad manners, and the immorality of the West . . . ; but who can tell the tale of those quiet lives which are the life-blood of the country,—its present strength and its hope of the future?"[1]

In her memoir, Mary Hallock Foote detailed the years she spent in mining towns observing the people, their ways of living and speaking. She found one of the miners' phrases particularly captivating. "The angle of repose" was, in her opinion, "too good to waste on rockslides or heaps of sand." She went on to explain that the phrase represented human life itself: "Each one of us in the Cañon was slipping and crawling and grinding along . . . towards that angle of repose which one finds and loses from time to time but is always seeking in one way or another."[2]

The "angle of repose" is the scientific term for the highest angle at which piles of sediment will remain at a state of rest—this angle varies for different types of materials, depending on the size and coarseness of the sand or rock. Wallace Stegner would adopt the phrase for the title of his Pulitzer-Prize-winning novel based heavily on the life and writings of Mary Hallock Foote. It is an apt phrase for a woman who spent her life writing and illustrating scenes from mining towns, where early excavation methods left discarded piles of tailings behind on abandoned sites. Surface tension and the force of gravity determines the slant at which these piles of material come to rest. Mary spent her life pulled by the equally powerful forces of east and west; of love and isolation; of inspiring beauty and grinding poverty—seeking to find the angle at which she could achieve balance and repose.

To open a volume of Mary's novels, autobiography, or correspondence is to be pulled into an incantatory dream. She writes with the pacing of a slow, languorous film—there is time, you feel, to revel in every aspect of the gradually unfolding scene. If Mary's descendants had not forbidden the creation of a movie based on the *Angle of Repose*,[3] Hollywood would probably shoot the film set in sweeping western vistas suffused with glowing light. In one of her most famous passages, she wrote, "There, in the whisper of the desert wind, it all comes back: The shiver of an old longing, and doubt and expectancy . . . the long, low house stretched out on the Mesa raised above the valley . . . the ring of mountains lifting and lowering down to the great gate where the sun is setting in a storm of gold. The purple shadows darken in their canons, the color mounts to the zenith, the plains are flushed with light."[4]

Mary made her living thanks to America's fascination with the West. Born in 1847 on a farm outside Milton, New York, she was raised in a large, close-knit Quaker family. Mary recalled accompanying her father "along the icy lanes in March, to see him feed cut-turnips to the yearling lambs."[5] He pointed to their shadows— stretched long by the light of the rising sun—and quoted the poet James Thomson: "Prepost'rous sight! The legs without the man." Mary did not recognize the quotation, but she never forgot the word *preposterous*, nor the light "streaming across the glistening fields," nor the lambs as her father "waded through their warm, bleating bodies to the barn."[6] These early experiences with the natural world awakened a sensitivity to beauty and description that Mary would draw upon for the rest of her life.

The Quaker community in which Mary was raised emphasized

education and equality of the sexes, so she enjoyed a childhood steeped in literature, rural landscape, and intellectual exchange. Her extended family included several preachers, and she enjoyed discussing religion and politics. In the evenings, her father often read editorials from *The New York Tribune* aloud. Mary's widowed aunt Sarah Hallock was a passionate reader and conversationalist; at her invitation, the family entertained many prominent visitors, including the famous abolitionist Frederick Douglass[7] and women's rights advocate Susan B. Anthony. Mary wrote, "They were brilliant talkers; all the villages in the valley of the Hudson and the Mohawk put together could not have furnished such conversation as we heard without stirring from our firesides."[8]

Mary received more education than many women of her day, initially attending a Quaker school set up by her father, and later the Poughkeepsie Female Collegiate Institute (the equivalent of high school). Mary started drawing at a young age and always enjoyed art. At the Institute, she took her first formal lessons. Upon seeing Mary's early efforts, Aunt Sarah declared Mary to be very talented and advised her to receive training in illustration. Sarah's opinion held weight in the family, so a few weeks before Mary's seventeenth birthday, she left for the School of Design for Women at the Cooper Union in New York City, one of the few places in the country at the time where women could be educated as artists.

Mary started art school not long after the outbreak of the Civil War. The conflict claimed the lives of three of her cousins, as well as the brother of her best friend, Helena. But in spite of the chaos playing out on battlefields, college was a miraculous awakening for the young artist. Coming from a rural community, for the first time she had access to a large library and classmates interested in heady intellectual discussion. Mary fell in love with the vibrancy of New York society and later wrote, "I remember only being absolutely well and gloriously happy all those months." Early in her schooling, she met Helena de Kay. The girls became inseparable. Sharing a deep love of literature as well as art, they forged a friendship that would remain influential throughout both of their lives. The young women shared projects, books, dreams for the future, and hours of discussion about women's role in art and society. Mary wrote, "Helena dawned on my nineteenth year like a rose pink winter sunrise. . . . Across the city we came together and across the world in some respects." Many years later Mary wrote her friend: "[It is useless] for me to begin to tell you how I love you, how I revel in your brightness when you are here, and what a blank you leave behind."[9]

As her social and intellectual life expanded, so did her artistic talent. Mary excelled in the medium of wood cut illustration, a popular illustration style for black and white magazines of the day. This artistic process involves engraving an image on a wood block with metal tools before the block is inked and printed onto paper. Because the artist creates a mirror image of the composition, wood cut illustration requires a strong sense of design and the ability to conceptualize the image in reverse. While at school, Mary won an award for being "the most meritorious pupil in drawing," and her drawings began appearing in *Galaxy Magazine*. One early critic called Hallock "a young artist whose compositions contain promise of no ordinary kind."[10] By 1871, Mary had received several commissions from *Galaxy, Scribner's,* and *Hearth and Home*. After graduation, she returned home, where her illustration income contributed to family finances. Many early illustrations featured domestic scenes—a kitten at play, girls ice skating on a pond; she often used sister and friends as models. Exhilarated by early success, Mary visited New York to meet with publishers. She admitted feeling "considerably puffed up after my drawings began to sell, with that pride of independence which was a new thing to daughters of that period."[11]

Both Mary and Helena dreamed of successful art careers, and the new graduates made plans to open a studio together in New York. To Helena's disappointment, Mary decided against the studio venture, partially due to disapproval from her family, partially because she made the acquaintance of Arthur Foote—a handsome young engineer educated at Yale. The two met at a mutual friend's Christmas gathering and became infatuated, though Foote returned to California for two years to continue training. They sent letters back and forth and Mary confessed, "We were not supposed to be engaged, but more and more through letters, as time went on, the tentative relation began to take hold upon one like an undertow."[12]

Helena also soon met her husband, Richard Gilder, an editor at *Scribner's*, though Helena wavered on the topic of marriage, concerned it would interfere with her artistic career. Gilder responded with adoring poetry (which he later published) and at last convinced her she could do both. They married and Helena delivered their first baby shortly before Arthur returned from California. During Arthur's absence, Mary threw herself into her illustration work, determined "to keep from becoming one of that dismal army of waiting women."[13] She received several important commissions, including a set of illustrations to accompany Longfellow's poetry. When *The New York Times* reviewed the work, they said her drawings were "as full of poetry and feeling as Mr. Longfellow's lines." Mary met the famous poet at a reception in New York, which left her dazzled by his positive reception. Next invited to illustrate *The Scarlet Letter* by Nathaniel Hawthorne, Mary went on to complete covers and interiors for many well-known magazines.

When Arthur returned, the couple exchanged vows in a simple Quaker ceremony before departing on a brief honeymoon in New York along the seashore. All too soon, Arthur returned to California, and Mary soon followed. Struggling with the emotion of leaving home, she wrote to Helena, "I confess to a longing to see this wonderful new world," but anticipation made separating from family, her artistic community, and dear friends no less excruciating. Initially, Mary planned to be away for two years. In reality, the Footes were gone for fifty-six, though Mary visited New York at regular intervals. Near the end of her life, Mary wrote, "No girl ever wanted less to 'go West' with any man, or paid a man a greater compliment by doing so."

Over the next five decades, Mary and Arthur moved around the West as he established his career. A brilliant engineer, Arthur proved a less successful businessman and had a difficult time working with others. His ideas frequently required large investments of capital that he failed to secure. The couple moved to San Jose, California; Leadville, Colorado; Deadwood, South Dakota; Boise, Idaho; and Morelia, Mexico; and three children were born along the way. Many of Arthur's engineering projects involved mining operations, so they frequently settled in rough mining towns, often in primitive log cabins. The life could not have been in greater contrast to the one to which Mary had grown accustomed. She wrote, "If I opened a trunk and took out a dress that had hung in the closets at home, waves of a faint, sickish emotion went over me. . . . I could have cried with the pang of those odors released from its folds."[14]

In spite of the rough environment, Mary retained her eastern manners, dressing in elegant fabrics and styles rarely seen in frontier towns. As her husband's career stalled several times, Mary's illustration work sustained the family. She employed a governess to educate her children, as well as a cook, so that she might continue her career, though Mary loved being a mother and, like many Victorian women, believed motherhood was the crowning achievement of a woman's life. That she missed her glittering life in the East is clear. In a story she wrote for *Century Magazine,* Mary wrote, "The life of the men may be large and dramatic, even in failure; but the life of women, here, as everywhere, is made up of very small matters. . . . It is the little shocks for which one is never prepared, the little disappointments and insecurities and failures and postponements, the want of completeness and perfection in anything, that harrows a woman's soul and makes her forget, too often, that she has a soul."[15]

Though Mary found life in the West challenging, in many ways it actually benefitted her career. The rough settlements were locations of great interest to East Coast publications. As a firsthand witness to mining towns and the landscapes of the West, Mary's audience trusted the authenticity of her observations. In addition to illustration work, Mary also began writing—first short stories for *Scribner's Magazine,* accompanied by illustrations; then novels, many of them drawn from her own experience, set in frontier towns with female protagonists. She said, "The East constantly hears of the recklessness, the bad manners, and the immorality of the West, just as England hears of all our disgraces, social, financial and national; but who can tell the tale of those quiet lives which are the life-blood of the country,—its present strength and its hope of the future?"[16]

Apparently, she could. Mary's books eventually would number twelve novels and four volumes of short stories, plus numerous magazine stories and essays; her published illustrations number in the hundreds. Eventually her own fame and Arthur's work helped bridge her feelings of isolation as their reputation lured famous visitors to their doorstep, drawn by the enticement of warm food and interesting conversation.

It is fair criticism that part of Mary's isolation was due to a socioeconomic status quite different from the working class people in mining towns; both Mary and Arthur have been accused of a fair amount of intellectual snobbery. Mary's biographer acknowledges that her writings were "skewed by an upper-class social bias that equated goodness and respectability with culture and education."[17]

In spite of an upper-class slant, Mary's novels and illustrations are accomplished works of art on their own merits. The fact that they present a portrait of mining towns in frontier America from the female perspective makes them even more valuable.

For a modern reader, she evokes the long-gone time and place. In one story she wrote, "If one possessed an ear-trumpet . . . by laying it on almost any spot of these steeply mounting hills and winding trails, one might hear the ringing of hammer and drill against the rock, the rumbling of cars through cavernous drifts, the dull thunder of blasts, even the voices of men burrowing in the heart of the mountain." In another story she described watching miners descend into the depths of the earth: "The great wheels of the engine slowly swing round and the heads disappear down the black hole. I can see a hand waved and the glimmer of a candle for a little way. The spark grows fainter and a warm, damp wind blows up the shaft."[18] Her words cast a slow spell upon the reader—leaving no doubt about why the West has long held such a fixation in the mind of the American imagination.

Mary also began writing western novels, though writing in such a traditionally male-dominated genre left her self-conscious and insecure. In a quote that is highly ironic given the controversy of later years, she confided, "How I wish I had a son who would put his name to my stories. One could write so much better if one were not a woman. . . . The fields beyond where only men may tread. I know as much about the men who tread those fields as a man could—more."[19] Luckily, critical response to her western novels remained far more generous than her own. Charles Lummis, contemporary literary critic, wrote that her novels were "marked by all the instincts

at once of woman, artist, poet, and story-teller, *The Led-Horse Claim*
and its fellows are of a quality that refuses to be forgotten."[20]

Some of the most challenging years for the Foote family took
place in Boise Canyon where Arthur envisioned a Boise River irrigation project; the idea eventually grew into an obsession. For ten
years, he relentlessly pursued the goal—but failed to raise sufficient
capital. Eventually forced to abandon the project, he descended into
depression and alcoholism, and Mary's writing and illustration remained their only source of income. The couple's third child arrived,
and the combination of childbirth and marital strain left Mary exhausted; it was one of the most unproductive periods of her life.
Eventually Arthur acknowledged defeat, and the family moved in
with Mary's sister Bessie, who at the time lived in Boise. With the
support of extended family and a new direction, both Mary and
Arthur improved greatly, and Mary returned to the work she loved.
The passage of time had vindicated Arthur's vision, and the project
he conceived during those difficult years later became the federal
government's Arrowrock Dam, which implemented most of Arthur's
original design.

Like many writers, Mary used her fiction as a place to explore
struggles drawn directly from her own life, and her fiction is filled
with the tension between the east and the west. In one short story,
she criticized gentlemen who found a "pretty girl" and lured her
west, though a "less expensive choice [would] fit the conditions
of their lives so much better." The voice of a woman now well-
acquainted with the ups and downs of marriage can be heard in her
reflection: "Between them both, the girl who expects to have a good
time, and the young man who is confident that he can give it to
her, there will probably be a good deal to learn."[21] Though marriage
to Arthur involved many challenges, she loved him and remained
proud of his integrity and hard work. Her autobiography records,

"My poor man . . . would ride through half a mile of dead hopes, dead trees and fields he had planted . . . but he brought himself—everything he had to give, including his patience and indomitable pluck. When he had a salary, it was 'ours'—when he had debts, they were 'his,' and paid them doggedly, year after year."[22]

Mary persisted in believing that one day Arthur would be successful. Though it took twenty years, eventually her prediction came to pass. In 1895, they moved to Grass Valley, California, where Arthur designed an electric-generating plant for the North Star Mine. He went on to create the North Star Mine Powerhouse, the world's largest operating impulse turbine wheel, which functioned for thirty years. Financially secure at last, the family built a beautiful home in Grass Valley designed by famed architect Julia Morgan. Mary continued writing and illustrating, composing the novel *Edith Bonham* in honor of Helena. Though financial challenges lay behind them, sorrow took a new form when the couple's beloved daughter Agnes died of appendicitis at age seventeen. Mary described her daughter as "stillness with love and day with light"[23] and covered Agnes's casket with Banksia roses from her yard. Each year when the blossoms reappeared, she gathered them and brought them to the grave. In 1919, Mary wrote *The Ground-Swell* in memory of Agnes.

Mary finally returned to the East in 1932, one year before Arthur passed away. In the last words of her autobiography, she acknowledged that she may have glossed over her own faults in its pages. "These fragments of my past are presented in a selected light and seen from a certain point of view. To that extent I suppose I am still the artist I tried to be, and the old romancer too. And everyone knows the magic perspectives of memory—it keeps what we loved and alters the relative size and value of many things that we did not love enough—that we hated and resisted and made mountains of at the time. It turns the dust of our valleys of humiliation, now that the sun of our working hours has set, into a sad and dreamy splendor which will fade into depths beyond depths of unknown worlds of stars."[24]

In the years following Foote's death, her work and memory did indeed fade, and her life became largely forgotten. Wallace Stegner discovered her oeuvre when one of his students began writing his dissertation on Foote. Though the student abandoned the dissertation topic, Mary's story captivated Stegner, and he contacted her descendants for permission to write a book based loosely on her life. That book became *Angle of Repose,* which won the Pulitzer Prize for fiction in 1972. Many reviewers commented on the authenticity of the female character Stegner "created," but the novel ultimately embroiled the author's name in controversy. Foote's family opposed the way in which he used some elements of her life but twisted and misrepresented others.[25] After the novel, the release of Mary's autobiography and correspondence created an even bigger controversy in the literary world when it became clear that extensive portions of Mary's writings were placed in Stegner's novel verbatim—whole paragraphs lifted directly from her work now appeared in a novel with Stegner's name on the front cover. Though Stegner promised the family early on in the project that the book "would involve no recognizable characterizations and no quotations direct from the letters," in fact, ten percent of the novel is taken from material directly written by Foote.[26]

As a writer, I can understand Stegner's use of Mary's life and the historical events surrounding them; historical events frequently serve as inspiration for fiction and many times require bending to suit fictional needs. But the appropriation of her voice and writing without even a footnote to acknowledge the words as Mary's own seems reprehensible. It's hard to imagine any other word for this besides plagiarism. Perhaps most alarming of all is Stegner's dismissal of Foote's significant contributions; he deemed her an unworthy subject of biography because "she did not strike me as important enough historically to make her more than modestly interesting."[27] Three biographies now exist about Foote, by the way, none of them authored by Stegner.[28]

The controversy has remained mainly in the academic world, since Foote's family, though deeply frustrated, decided against litigation, but a third writer has brought some degree of reconciliation to the conflict. In the 2001 play entitled *Fair Use* by Sands Hall, Stegner and Foote share a stage and she is given a chance to respond to Stegner's use of her life's work. Their dialogue is a conversation that never happened on this earth, but the play explores the complex issue of creative authority and lends a fitting resolution to the broader tale. The play quotes many of Foote's descriptions of the West, and "in the end . . . Foote's own words make clear she did not need Wallace Stegner to make her immortal."[29]

I picture Mary silhouetted against the landscape of the West, angled against the horizon—engaged, yet at peace, reclining, yet alert—held motionless at a perfect angle of repose. Mary's life illuminates the challenges women have faced throughout history as they have sought to cultivate their own voices and fight appropriation by dominant forces. Her life also illustrates many of the demands women struggle to reconcile in any age. Though I doubt she felt it at the time, from my perspective Mary managed to create astounding equilibrium through the balancing of these competing forces: she found time for herself while maintaining relationships with her family; she managed to prioritize both her work as a mother and her work as an artist. She believed in and stood by those she loved no

matter how many times they failed. In the midst of making significant sacrifices for her husband's career, she did not lose sight of her
own. Even in harsh circumstances, she continued to do the work she
found both valuable and rewarding.

Mary's life renews my commitment to my own interests and passions. She is a reminder not to minimize your own accomplishments,
nor to allow others to do it for you. Certainly, her story speaks today
as both a reminder to give fair credit for inspiration drawn from
others and to not allow others to take credit for that which you have
created. Her life is an inducement to find balance between action
and rest; company and solitude; outward and inward dimensions—
an invitation to create your own harmony from the competing tensions of your life and discover your own angle of repose.

FURTHER READING

Lee Ann Johnson, *Mary Hallock Foote* (Woodbridge, CT: Twayne Publishers,
1980).

Darlis A. Miller, *Mary Hallock Foote: Author-Illustrator of the American West*
(Norman: University of Oklahoma Press, 2002).

Susan Cummins Miller, *A Sweet, Separate Intimacy: Women Writers of the American
Frontier, 1800–1922* (Salt Lake City: University of Utah Press, 2000).

Rodman W. Paul, ed., *A Victorian Gentlewoman in the Far West: The Reminiscences
of Mary Hallock Foote* (San Marino, CA: Huntington Library Press, 1972).

NOTES

1. *Scribner's Monthly: An Illustrated Magazine for the People,* conducted by F. G. Holland. Volume XVI
(New York: Scribner & Co., New York, 1878), 460.

2. Rodman W. Paul, ed., *A Victorian Gentlewoman in the Far West: The Reminiscences of Mary Hallock
Foote* (San Marino, CA: Huntington Library Press, 1972), 306, 309.

3. The family forbade the film adaptation of the novel as part of the Wallace Stegner controversy
mentioned later in this chapter.

4. Accessed online at http://articles.latimes.com/2003/mar/23/magazine/tm-stegner12/6.

5. Paul, *Victorian Gentlewoman,* 51.

6. Ibid., 52.

7. It is clear that the family was highly progressive for their time. In fact, Mary notes in her memoirs

that when Douglass came to visit the Hallock family, their Irish servant girl refused to serve him (see Paul, *Victorian Gentlewoman*, 54).

8. Darlis A. Miller, *Mary Hallock Foote: Author-Illustrator of the American West* (Norman: University of Oklahoma Press, 2002), 8.

9. Ibid., 23.

10. Ibid., 19.

11. Ibid., 22.

12. Paul, *Victorian Gentlewoman*, 101.

13. Miller, *Mary Hallock Foote, Author-Illustrator*, 29.

14. Paul, *Victorian Gentlewoman*, 132.

15. Lillian Schlissel and Catherine J. Lavender, "Pretty Girls in the West," in *The Western Women's Reader* (New York: HarperPerennial, 2000), 214.

16. *Scribner's Monthly*, 460.

17. Miller, *Mary Hallock Foote, Author-Illustrator*, 40.

18. Mary Hallock Foote, "A California Mining Camp," in Susan Cummins Miller, *A Sweet, Separate Intimacy: Women Writers of the American Frontier, 1800–1922* (Salt Lake City: University of Utah Press, 2000), 220–21.

19. Lee Ann Johnson, *Mary Hallock Foote* (Woodbridge, CT: Twayne Publishers, 1980), 116.

20. Ibid., 113.

21. Schlissel and Lavender, "Pretty Girls in the West," 214.

22. Paul, *Victorian Gentlewoman*, 344.

23. Ibid., 397.

24. Ibid., 400.

25. In Stegner's novel, "Susan" (the character based on Mary) falls out of love with her husband and has a brief affair with one of her husband's colleagues. Stegner also portrayed Susan's relationship with the character Helena as potentially homosexual.

26. Susan Salter Reynolds, "Tangle of Repose," *LA Times*, March 23, 2003. Accessed online at http://articles.latimes.com/2003/mar/23/magazine/tm-stegner12/6.

27. Ibid.

28. The biographies mentioned are *Mary Hallock Foote: Author-Illustrator of the American West* by Darlis A. Miller; *Mary Hallock Foote* by Lee Ann Johnson; and *Mary Hallock Foote: Pioneer Woman Illustrator* by Doris Bickford-Swarthout (N.p.: Berry Hill Press, 1996). Of the three, the first is by far the most comprehensive.

29. Reynolds, "Tangle of Repose."

CHAPTER 9

MARTHA HUGHES CANNON
FRONTIER DOCTOR AND FIRST FEMALE STATE SENATOR

Born: July 1, 1857, Llandudno, Wales
Died: July 10, 1932, Los Angeles, California

"Mrs. Doctor Martha Hughes Cannon . . . is one of the brightest exponents of the women's cause in the United States."[1]

At the Chicago World's Fair of 1893, where Tesla dazzled crowds with the first electric light displays, where spray paint and the Ferris Wheel both made their world debuts, a female doctor delivered an impassioned speech on behalf of women's rights. To the assembled crowd, this eloquent physician declared, "One of the principal reasons why women should vote is that all men and women are created free and equal. No privileged class either of sex, wealth, or descent should be allowed to arise or exist. All persons should have the legal right to be the equal of every other."[2] Listeners marveled at her message, as dazzling and borrowed from the future as Tesla's lights. What made the speech all the more surprising was the knowledge that in addition to her other accomplishments, the speaker was Dr. Martha Hughes Cannon, the fourth polygamous wife of a prominent Mormon leader from the territory of Utah.

The life of Martha Hughes Cannon is filled with dualities and contradictions. Unafraid of a male-dominated world, she unabashedly competed on both the local and national stages as a brilliant and educated physician and scholar. Yet she was also a mother of three children and a polygamist. As a successful politician and advocate for women's rights, Martha held the public stage; yet she spent several years hiding with her children under an assumed identity. Her life defies simple categorization, though she certainly deserved the praise of one contemporary, Judge Orlando Powers, who called her "a brave and brilliant woman."[3]

Martha was born into religious controversy. As the second of three daughters born in North Wales, Martha was two years old when her parents joined The Church of Jesus Christ of Latter-day Saints, a highly contested religion at that time. Because of persecution, the couple chose to be baptized in the river Llamrust in the middle of the night. Afraid their parents would attempt to take their children by force, Martha's parents swiftly sold their possessions and joined other Church members in Liverpool, England. In 1860, they sailed for America.

It was a difficult ocean crossing. Young Mattie, as Martha was often called, dealt with constant seasickness, and her father's health declined. Though they hoped to travel to Utah, the family settled temporarily in New York, where Mattie's mother worked in a tie-making factory and took in washing. When the Civil War broke out, it seemed unlikely the Hughes family would be able to leave; however, in 1861, they joined a Church-sponsored group traveling by train to Nebraska, then overland by wagon to Salt Lake City.

With her husband in poor health and three little girls under the age of five, Elizabeth Hughes walked every step of the journey to Utah. Long before they reached Salt Lake, Elizabeth's shoes gave out completely; she tied rags over the remnants and continued walking. It's difficult to imagine the demands of such a trip as the vast majority of the burden fell upon Elizabeth's shoulders. Two weeks before the end of the trail, the youngest daughter, one-year-old Annie, passed away. The family buried their child in an unmarked grave and continued west with grief-stricken hearts. The company arrived in the Salt Lake Valley on the thirteenth of September, but three days later, Peter Hughes joined his daughter in death. Even into adulthood, Mattie remembered the tall figure of her father stretched out in a coffin.

Though very young, Mattie was acutely influenced by the events of her early life. The sacrifices her parents made for their religion left a deep impression on her. She would later say, "My parents were Mormon. I am a Mormon." She bore testimony of the impact faith had upon her life: "I have seen the power of God made manifest in my behalf, for which I feel to thank Him every day of my life."[4] Though the sacrifices she made to follow her religion would be very different, they would be no less trying. Additionally, the physical suffering Mattie witnessed on the trail, including the deaths of her baby sister and father, impacted her deeply. Alleviating physical suffering seemed to Mattie a goal worth the dedication of one's life.

A year after arriving in Salt Lake, Mattie's mother married a man named James Patton Paul, a widower with four sons. The blended family that involved Elizabeth's two girls, James's four sons, and the five new children they had together was surely chaotic, but it was also successful. According to Mattie's great-granddaughter, Elizabeth frequently said in jest, "*Your* children and *my* children are abusing *our* children."[5] Mattie formed a close relationship with her stepfather. He recognized her intelligence, even though she was young, and encouraged her to pursue her dreams, believing she was capable of accomplishment far beyond the typical role of women in Victorian society. When she raised the possibility of becoming a doctor, James applauded her ambition. To show gratitude for his influence, Mattie adopted his last name, going by Mattie Hughes Paul.

Mattie worked toward her goal with astounding deliberation. She began teaching elementary school at age fourteen and landed a job as a typesetter for the *Deseret News* at age fifteen. Accepted at the University of Deseret (modern-day University of Utah), she majored in chemistry. Near the end of her schooling in Salt Lake, she successfully completed a grueling exam that excused her from the first two years of medical school.[6] She paid for her own education by working as a typesetter for the influential *Woman's Exponent,* a newspaper published by the LDS women's organization. Working at the newspaper brought her into contact with eloquent words and the intellectual discussions of the day; several prominent women at the *Exponent* encouraged Mattie, recognizing her intelligence and ambition.

When Brigham Young originally led a group of displaced pioneers to the Salt Lake Valley, the Mormons had hoped to establish a community where they could practice their religious lifestyle in peace. With the arrival of the transcontinental railroad in Salt Lake City in 1869 and the development of the mining industry, an increasing number of secular settlers arrived in the valley, creating tension between the two groups. As the city grew, the debate over the role the Church should play in public life evolved. In order to build a self-sufficient community, the LDS Church asked members to seek education and professional training in the East. Women healers were common in the community, and Mattie was not only encouraged in her desire to be trained as a doctor but was also "set apart"[7] by Church leaders for the experience.

Mattie became known for benign yet quirky tendencies during these years. She walked six miles a day to school, often through the snow and slush of Salt Lake winters. Finding traditional women's fashion impractical, she cut her hair very short, claiming that long hair was unhealthy. She pinned up her long skirts so they wouldn't get wet and bought a pair of men's work boots. Once she arrived at school, Mattie unpinned her skirts and changed her shoes, but she wasn't one to be fussy about frivolous conventions.

This attitude served her well when it came to attending medical school. Though she could have opted for one of the female schools of the day, Mattie chose the University of Michigan, a top-tier school that had only begun allowing females five years previously. Shortly before her departure, the *Women's Exponent* noted, "She has educated herself by her own energy, industry, and economy. . . . Her example of diligence and perseverance is worthy of imitation. Miss Paul is a young lady of exceptional ability and deserves to succeed."[8] Mattie stepped into the world of medical school, where all her professors and the vast majority of her peers were male. Though medical schools technically allowed women at that time, in reality, female students faced great challenges, and many male professors refused to discuss anatomy if women were in the room. Female students were often forced to observe from an annex area outside the regular classroom, and they endured social isolation as well. Disregarding these difficulties, Mattie graduated from medical school at age twenty-three, the only female in a class of seventy-five physicians. She said of her graduation day (which happened to fall on her birthday): "It was my day of days. With 204 other graduates, I marched triumphantly onto the great platform where we were presented with our diplomas amidst the cheers of the crowded hall."[9]

Not content with this enormous accomplishment, Mattie continued her education at the University of Pennsylvania, where she studied the latest research on germ theory and earned a bachelor of science degree in pharmacology. She also studied at the National School of Elocution and Oratory, with the goal of strengthening her public speaking skills so that she would be able to address audiences on issues of public health. She had a flair for the dramatic, and some of her instructors and peers tried to persuade her to leave the medical profession career for acting instead. During her time at the oratory school, Mattie became close friends with classmate Barbara

Replogle; the two friends remained close throughout their lives and maintained a regular correspondence.[10] Armed with a vast amount of knowledge and education, Dr. Mattie Hughes returned to Utah.

Mattie's stepfather Paul continued to be one of her strongest supporters. To celebrate her return, he built an extension on their home for a medical office. She set up practice and purchased a horse and buggy for house calls. Doctors were still very rare in frontier Utah, particularly female doctors as well-educated as Mattie now was. Though medicine had advanced, many doctors still practiced blood-letting and operated with fabricated credentials. Mattie soon had many patients.

Mattie was in the process of developing her private practice when the board of the newly created Deseret Hospital invited Mattie to be their resident physician. She accepted the invitation and established classes for midwives, where she lectured on obstetrics. Angus Munn Cannon, a prominent LDS leader, was one member of the hospital's board of directors.[11] There are two variations of the first meeting between Angus and Mattie. In one, Mattie instructed Angus to leave a hospital room so she could continue her work. In the second, she was cleaning the hospital's front porch when Angus blocked her path and she ordered him out of the way.[12] Regardless of which story is correct, they met and Angus clearly found her independent nature attractive. In 1884, she would become his fourth polygamous wife.

A woman as intelligent and ambitious as Mattie had no shortage of suitors. In fact, she broke off an engagement before departing for medical school, and one suitor in Michigan converted to Mormonism and followed her back to Salt Lake! Why such a woman would choose to become the fourth polygamous wife of a man twenty-three years her senior is part of the contradiction of Mattie's life. Perhaps it initially seemed exciting and flattering—Angus was well respected and held a high position of authority in the LDS Church. They told no one about the marriage. Even Mattie's parents were not invited to the ceremony. Strict secrecy was necessary because the United States government had become increasingly opposed to polygamy; in fact, Angus was already under investigation by federal authorities when he married Mattie.

That they loved each other deeply is without question. Although Mattie's personal journals were burned at her request, the correspondence between Mattie and Angus remains—constituting hundreds of letters written during the course of their marriage. Angus wrote in his journal, "I gazed upon Martha and felt that she was grown for me." In spite of the avalanche of anguish that married life brought, Mattie wrote, "I am proud of my choice. I would rather spend one hour in your society than a whole lifetime with any man I know of."[13]

Unfortunately, Mattie and Angus could not have entered into polygamy at a more difficult time. The LDS Church began practicing polygamy in Illinois and Missouri in the 1840s. Due to clashes with their neighbors over a variety of issues, including their anti-slavery stance in the pro-slavery state of Missouri, they were eventually driven from both of these states. In Utah, polygamy was openly supported by Church membership as a whole, though only around 25 to 30 percent of the members lived in polygamy in the late 1800s. By the end of the century the number dropped to ten percent, most commonly practiced among Church leadership. As the boundaries of the United States pushed farther west, controversy over the religion and the practice of polygamy followed them. Abraham Lincoln was too busy fighting the Civil War to worry about Mormons on the western borders. He said, "Tell Brigham Young that if he will leave me alone, I'll leave him alone."[14]

After the war, however, as more settlers arrived in the area, the issue once again became a topic of debate, and Congress passed several acts of legislation intended to make the practice more difficult. Federal marshals in Utah offered monetary rewards for turning in their neighbors, while agents broke into houses, peeped into windows, and pumped children for information about their family living arrangements. Members fled to Canada and Mexico, went into hiding, and created an underground railroad to help practicioners escape imprisonment. In May of 1885, Angus was sentenced to six months in prison and fined three hundred dollars. Before a judge Angus testified, "I can only say that I have used the utmost of my power to honor my God, my family, and my country. I did not think I would be found a criminal for that."[15] When Angus was arrested, Mattie was five months pregnant.

Mattie became a highly sought after individual. The courts wanted her to testify against her husband as well as other polygamous families whose babies she had delivered. Unwilling to testify against her friends and family, Mattie went into hiding, forced to abandon her medical practice for the time being. She gave birth to a daughter in the house of a friend while Angus remained in prison. Mattie wrote to Angus, "I would rather be a stranger in a strange land than a sneaking captive at home,"[16] and the thought of safety among friends and relatives in Wales and England soon drew her overseas.

Time abroad held both joy and pain. Mattie marveled at the sights of Paris and Stratford-on-Avon but grew frustrated by her inability to use the medical training she had worked so hard to acquire. Angus married his fifth wife just days before Mattie departed from the country, a fact that made the time emotionally painful as well. While in England, Mattie's daughter Lizzie accidentally drank some ammonia and nearly died. Mattie wrote, "I believe positively I should have gone mad had [Elizabeth] been taken."[17]

After two years abroad, Mattie returned to the United States.

Angus met her in New York and they spent several happy days together. Back in Utah, Mattie began practicing medicine again, establishing the first nurses' training school in Salt Lake City. Though Mattie had hoped the polygamy controversy would die down while she was away, in many ways things only became worse. In 1887, Congress passed the Edumunds–Tucker Act, which disenfranchised all Utah women, dissolved the LDS Church as a legal entity, and gave federal officials the right to seize Church property and assets, including the partially constructed Salt Lake temple.

As a fourth wife, this legislation declared Mattie's children illegitimate. It also highly impacted her financial situation—she would not inherit any of her husband's estate. Finally, it meant she could never live openly with her husband, as only the first wife could appear with her husband publicly. Mattie defended the practice of plural marriage openly all her life, but there is no question it caused her great suffering. At times in her letters, she stated the practice was ordained by God, while other times she was consumed by jealousy at the thought of her husband's other wives. Above all, her heart broke for the fact that she could not live freely with the man she loved. "Oh for a home," she wrote. "For a husband of my own because he is my own. A father for my children whom they know by association. . . . Will they ever be enjoyed by this storm-tossed exile?"[18]

As Congress debated a bill that would remove voting rights from all members of the Church,[19] Wilford Woodruff revealed a "Manifesto" officially discontinuing the practice of polygamy, which eased the pressure from the government at last. Though some polygamous marriages continued to be performed in secret, the federal government assumed correctly that the practice would die out naturally, and the situation became much more bearable for Mattie. She returned to Salt Lake with her two children and went back to work. She wrote to her friend Barbara, "I feel that the spark of ambition is not yet dead within, but smolders ready to burst into flame when the legitimate opportunity presents itself."[20]

The opportunity presented itself as Utah petitioned again for statehood amidst a debate as to whether women's suffrage should be included in the request. Utah and Wyoming were the first two territories to give women the vote, and, in fact, women in Utah had enjoyed the privilege for seventeen years before finding it rescinded by the Edmunds–Tucker Act. Mattie joined the suffragists and became a leader in the Utah chapter of the National Woman Suffrage Association, delivering speeches throughout Utah and participating in national conferences. Invited to speak at the 1893 Chicago World's Fair, she also appeared before a congressional committee in Washington, D.C., to report on the effect of women's suffrage in Utah. Now, at last, her oratory studies paid off. Before the congressional committee she stated, "[Woman] can, when allowed to do so, become a most powerful and a most potent factor in the affairs of the government. . . . Woman suffrage is no longer an experiment, but is a practical reality, tending to the well-being of the State."[21] Everywhere she spoke, this accomplished doctor dazzled listeners, challenging their preconceived notions about polygamist frontier wives. The *Chicago Record* stated, "Mrs. Doctor Martha Hughes Cannon . . . is one of the brightest exponents of the women's cause in the United States."[22]

The acceptance of Utah to statehood in 1896, with women's suffrage on the constitution, caused great celebration. Susan B. Anthony traveled to Utah to share the victory with her Utah sisters. Anxious not to anger the government, the LDS Church encouraged members to split their votes evenly between the two parties, which worked out for the Cannons, as Angus was a staunch Republican and Mattie registered as a Democrat. Now that women had the vote, their involvement in politics became the obvious next step.

In assembling the legislature for the first state senate elections, the Republican party collected a list of names, including Angus M. Cannon and Emmeline B. Wells. Within a few days, the Democratic party approached Mattie and asked her to run on their ticket; when she accepted, she was unaware that Angus had been nominated to represent the Republicans.

Though they weren't directly running against each other, the media had a field day with the idea of a prominent leader like Angus running for office in the same election as his wife. The *Salt Lake Tribune* called for a public debate between the two, saying, "What would draw a bigger crowd, to whom the truths of democracy might be expounded, than the prospect of a public verbal set-to between Dr. Mattie Hughes Cannon and her husband, Angus M. Cannon?"[23] Not surprisingly, the debate never happened. As the election drew near, Mattie claimed the situation did not bother either party involved, though some sources indicate the situation caused some marital strain. The *Salt Lake Herald* advised its voters, "Angus M. Cannon is a worthy man. . . . Against him we haven't a word to say. Only we would say that Mrs. Mattie Hughes Cannon, his wife, is the better man of the two. Send Mrs. Cannon to the state senate as a Democrat and let Mr. Cannon as a Republican remain at home to manage home industry."[24]

The election was very close. Only 2,671 votes separated the Republicans from the Democrats, but when officials counted the ballots, the Democrats had won. Thus Mattie beat her husband and became the first woman ever to hold the office of state senator in the United States,[25] twenty-four years before most women in the United States could vote! Publicly Mattie insisted that her husband didn't care about the defeat, and Angus himself said, "I feel proud of my Welsh wife."[26]

Mattie served two terms as state senator. At last she had the opportunity to combine several of her passions on a public stage; she swiftly moved to introduce legislation focused on improving public health. She championed a law that provided educational services for children with disabilities and another for better work conditions for female employees. Mattie helped establish the Utah State Board of Health to increase sanitation in overcrowded Salt Lake City. She supported a pure food law, protected the State Board of Public Examiners, and assisted with a bill to establish the first Art Institute in the country. Drawing on her study of bacteria, she discontinued the citywide practice of attaching metal cups to public drinking facilities, gaining the respect of those on both sides of the political spectrum. There was even talk of sending Mattie to Washington, when the collision of her public and private world exploded in controversy—once more, she became pregnant.

Part of the agreement of the Manifesto was that married men would no longer domestically cohabit with wives other than their first. Mattie's pregnancy was proof that she was disobeying this law, with far more significant consequences due to her role as a public servant. Her political career was effectually over. Officials arrested Angus and imposed a hundred-dollar fine in response to the scandal, and Mattie gave birth to baby Gwendolyn three weeks after her second senate term came to an end. In spite of the challenging sacrifices caused by the circumstances of the birth, Mattie adored her daughter. Because of Gwendolyn's bright and vivacious personality, Mattie called her the "darling of my heart."[27] She claimed she never regretted having the baby, in spite of the controversy. After the birth of Gwendolyn, Mattie retired from public office but continued practicing medicine, splitting her time between Pacific Grove, California, and Salt Lake City, Utah.

Following Angus's death in 1915, Mattie spent more time in California, where her children settled with families of their own. She volunteered at the Graves Medical Clinic and continued to research narcotic addictions. Mattie passed away in 1932 at age seventy-five and was buried beside Angus in the Salt Lake City Cemetery, finally achieving in death constant close proximity to her husband.

❧

It is not often one has the opportunity to use the words physician, polygamist, senator, exile, and women's rights advocate while describing the same person. Mattie defied easy categorization and in many ways remains an enigma. How I would love to read the personal journals that were burned by her request at her death; she chose to take her feelings about the events of her life to her grave. Though the situation Mattie faced is extreme and unusual, her struggle to balance motherhood and career is something women are still trying to work out a century later. Though she chose a marital path that was controversial and fraught with complications, she came to terms with the sacrifices the choice necessitated and handled it graciously. Mattie demonstrated an ability to funnel personal disappointments into other rewarding aspects of life as she made immense sacrifices to follow a faith she believed in and worked hard to leave the world better than she found it.

Perhaps more than anything, I admire Mattie's determination to pursue her ambitious goals and dreams. Working within a male-dominated world, she was not afraid to dream of the loftiest stage upon which to use her talents. Her thirst for knowledge and hard work carried her through years of study and preparation, which she then used to improve the world in ways she believed to be important. Her life exemplified the admonishment she once wrote to her friend Barbara: "Let us not waste our talents in the cauldron of modern nothingness but strive to become women of intellect, and endeavor to do some little good while we live in this protracted gleam called life."[28]

FURTHER READING

Mari Grana, *Pioneer, Polygamist, Politician: The Life of Dr. Martha Hughes Cannon* (Lanham, MD: TwoDot, 2009).

Christy Karras, *More Than Petticoats: Remarkable Utah Women* (Guilford, CT: Globe Pequot Press, 2010).

Constance L. Lieber, *Letters from Exile: The Correspondence of Martha Hughes Cannon and Angus M. Cannon, 1886–1888* (Salt Lake City: Signature Books, 1989).

Martha Hughes Cannon, DVD presentation (Salt Lake City: University of Utah Press, 2012).

Karen Surina Mulford, *Trailblazers: Twenty Amazing Western Women* (Flagstaff, AZ: Northland Publishing, 2001).

JoAnn A. Peterson (great-granddaughter of Martha Hughes Cannon), "The Life Story of Martha Maria Hughes (Paul) Cannon" (1985), manuscript in LDS Church History Library archives, Salt Lake City, Utah.

Richard E. Turley Jr. and Brittany A. Chapman, eds., *Women of Faith in the Latter Days, vol. 3, 1846–1870* (Salt Lake City: Deseret Book Co., 2014).

NOTES

1. Mari Grana, *Pioneer, Polygamist, Politician: The Life of Dr. Martha Hughes Cannon* (Lanham, MD: TwoDot, 2009), 80.

2. Ibid., 81.

3. Judge Orlando Powers said this of Martha after having the opportunity to work with her during her time as state senator. Though Judge Powers adamantly opposed polygamy, he was highly impressed with Martha. In particular, he was impressed that she represented a political party different from the one to which her husband belonged. He became even more impressed when she voted for a Democrat because she admired his character and positions on issues, in spite of the fact that he was well-known for expressing anti-Mormon sentiments.

4. Richard E. Turley Jr. and Brittany A. Chapman, eds., *Women of Faith in the Latter Days, vol. 3, 1846–1870* (Salt Lake City, UT: Deseret Book Co., 2014), 26.

5. JoAnn A. Peterson (great-granddaughter of Martha Hughes Cannon), "The Life Story of Martha Maria Hughes (Paul) Cannon" (1985), manuscript in LDS Church History Library archives, Salt Lake City, Utah.

6. Ibid., 5.

7. An LDS religious practice wherein hands are laid upon the head of the recipient and words of guidance, comfort, and counsel are spoken.

8. Peterson, "Life Story."

9. *Martha Hughes Cannon,* DVD presentation (Salt Lake City: University of Utah Press, 2012).

10. Turley and Chapman, *Women of Faith,* 14.

11. The highest administrative positions in the LDS Church are the First Presidency, followed by the Quorum of the Twelve Apostles.

12. Peterson, "Life Story."

13. *Martha Hughes Cannon*, DVD.

14. Grana, *Pioneer, Polygamist, Politician*, 81.

15. *History of the Bench and Bar of Utah* (Salt Lake City, UT: Interstate Press Association, 1913), 59.

16. Christy Karras, *More Than Petticoats: Remarkable Utah Women* (Guilford, CT: Globe Pequot Press, 2010), 80.

17. Cathy Luchetti, *Medicine Women: The Story of Early-American Women Doctors* (New York: Crown, 1998), 61.

18. Grana, *Pioneer, Polygamist, Politician*, 69.

19. The Cullom-Struble Bill.

20. Letter from Martha Hughes Cannon "To my loved Barbara," from Sussex, England, August 6, 1887, LDS Church History Library.

21. Hughes's testimony regarding women's suffrage before the House of Representatives, February 15, 1898, Hearing on House Joint Resolution 68 (rights of citizens to vote shall not be denied on account of sex).

22. Grana, *Pioneer, Polygamist, Politician*, 80.

23. Ibid., 87.

24. *Salt Lake Herald*, October 31, 1896.

25. Karen Surina Mulford, *Trailblazers: Twenty Amazing Western Women* (Flagstaff, AZ: Northland Publishing, 2001), 70.

26. Letter to Martha Hughes Cannon from Angus Cannon, May 25, 1903, LDS Church History Library.

27. *Martha Hughes Cannon*, DVD.

28. Letter from Martha Hughes Cannon to Barbara Repogle, May 1, 1885, LDS Church History Library.

CHAPTER 10

DONALDINA CAMERON
THE MOST LOVED AND FEARED WOMAN IN CHINATOWN

Born: July 26, 1869, New Zealand
Died: January 4, 1968, Palo Alto, California

> "If I had my life to live over again I'd do it the same way. Only I'd be better prepared."[1]

If you walk today down the crowded, narrow streets of San Francisco's Chinatown, you will find an imposing old building created from fire-warped bricks. The organization at 920 Sacramento Street runs youth programs, offers counseling services, and provides food and employment assistance to at-risk Asian communities. Known as the "Cameron House," this organization has existed since 1874, and is named after a brave and fearless crusader who was invited to teach a year of sewing lessons and ended up remaining for more than forty, fighting for the abolishment of a slave trade decades after the Civil War.

Donaldina Cameron rescued thousands of Chinese girls from sex trafficking rings, then raised them as her own daughters in the home at 920 Sacramento Street. Known to her girls as *Lo Mo,* the Chinese phrase means "old mama," a term that connotes both intimacy and respect. The slave traders and brothel owners, however, had another name for her: *Fahn Quai,* or "white devil."[2] Her daring rescue operations established her as one of the most loved and feared women in Chinatown.

Donaldina was born in 1869 in New Zealand to pioneering

Scottish parents on a sheep ranch in New Zealand. She was the adored baby of the family, with five older sisters and an older brother. Dedicated to each other and their Presbyterian faith, Donaldina's family remained close throughout their lives. Though she would be raised on tales of the Scottish highlands, she was two years old when her father decided to start over again in California, lured by reports of the state's lush pastureland. The family established a new sheep ranch, but tragedy struck when Isabella Cameron, Donaldina's mother, passed away. Her older sisters, ages eighteen and twenty, took good care of their youngest sister, however, forming a bond that would remain unbreakable.

Challenges continued as her father lost the ranch and the family moved several times. Donaldina attended high school in San Gabriel Valley and began her first year of college, planning to train as a teacher, but her father's unexpected death put an end to her college hopes. She became briefly engaged at age nineteen, but the relationship did not last. Looking for a new direction in life, Donaldina listened with horror and fascination as a friend's mother described her work helping protect Chinese girls who were sold naked on auction blocks in Chinatown. Donaldina immediately expressed interest in the work, and Mrs. Browne invited her to help. "I'm not educated for it," Donaldina protested, but Mrs. Browne persisted. "You can teach the girls to sew. Will you come for just one year?"[3] Donaldina decided to accept.

She arrived at 920 Sacramento Street, a world away from the Cameron family's home in the country. Thousands of people lived in the crowded San Francisco neighborhood of brick buildings mingled with Chinese pagodas and fish markets. Although in 1895 women's suffrage was making progress and African slavery had been abolished, life remained very difficult for the Chinese. Banned from public schools and courtrooms, they could not own property or live outside of the Chinese quarter except as servants; no path to citizenship existed. Chinese immigrants typically held the most dangerous and onerous jobs, laboring long hours for little pay in mines and factories. Frustrated by the lack of opportunity, many Chinese immigrants turned to dealing in underground business schemes instead. Opium, gambling, and prostitution were legal in China, so a thriving black market for these goods and services soon developed in Chinatown.

Increasingly stringent immigration laws made a challenging situation even worse. Exclusion laws prohibited Chinese men from sending for their wives, importing wives from China, or marrying non-Chinese women. At the time Donaldina arrived in San Francisco, men outnumbered women by twenty to one.[4] Desperately lonely, men were willing to pay hundreds and thousands of dollars for Chinese girls. Cultural misogyny only compounded the situation—female children held little value and were easily acquired from families in desperate financial circumstances. As a repressed gender within a repressed ethnic minority, Chinese women occupied the bottom of the social ladder in every respect. Corrupt San Francisco officials permitted, and in many cases complied with, the lucrative black market trade, and the word within the police department was that if you had bills to pay, you should get on the Chinatown beat.

A typical slave route to the United States began with a sale of a young girl in China for as little as ten dollars. Some sellers were financially desperate parents, while others were misled to believe their daughters would be educated or married. After being smuggled to San Francisco, girls as young as three often worked as *mui tsais,* or house servants, frequently enduring heavy labor and physical abuse. Once the girls reached the age of ten to twelve, they were sold into brothels or "cribs." In narrow alleyways, from behind barred windows, these captives were forced to call out their services to potential customers passing by. Some girls were chained to their beds; others were drugged. If they became ill, they were taken to a "hospital," which entailed a locked room where they would be left to starve to death. Within a few years, most girls in cribs contracted a venereal disease, died, or committed suicide.[5]

Before her arrival in San Francisco, Donaldina had lived a relatively sheltered life with a happy family, never comprehending the suffering that existed only miles from her home. Horrified by the situation she found in Chinatown, she threw herself into the work. "Because of my childhood family, I have a great deal of love," she said, "and I can pour it out."[6] She certainly did. Some of the girls responded immediately to Lo Mo's love and affection, but others, still struggling with opium addictions and trauma from severe abuse, took much longer. In fact, some chose to leave the mission home entirely and return to the streets. It was for these girls that Donaldina mourned the most.

One young resident of the home named Tien had been sold at the age of five to pay her father's gambling debts in China. In California, Tien did the washing and cleaning for the entire family with her owner's baby strapped to her back. If there was a problem with her work, her mistress pinched or burned her face with candle wax, which left permanent scars. Donaldina was captivated by the child and tried hard to win her trust, but Tien rejected all attempts at friendship and constantly broke the rules. After several months, an older girl Tien adored fell ill, and Tien hovered near the girl's bedside for weeks. One morning, the girl's face changed. Panicked, Tien called Donaldina, who instantly recognized the face of death; she sank beside the bed, sobbing in genuine grief. Tien, at last convinced of Donaldina's authenticity, wrapped her arms around her teacher. "Don't worry, Lo Mo. I help you," she said. The moment formed a dramatic turning point in their relationship, and soon the two were inseparable. Tien seldom left Donaldina's side after that experience and later served as her translator on raids.

Donaldina's year passed quickly and both the director of the house, the talented Margaret Culbertson, and the governing board begged her to stay. Donaldina requested a leave and spent time with her family, pondering her choices for the future. Chinatown was the last place she had imagined spending her life, and she hesitated to make a permanent commitment, but there was no question that she loved the girls and the work. She agreed to extend for a second year, but a few months into this period, Margaret Culbertson, who had run the home for sixteen years, passed away quite suddenly. Donaldina felt the weight of the house settle onto her very unprepared shoulders. Though the board invited her to become director, she insisted that she did not have enough experience, so another director was appointed, while Donaldina continued handling most of the day-to-day affairs of the house.

Organizing a house of fifty children in different stages of recovery was no easy task, but day-to-day routines provided stability. The girls rose early, dressed and bathed, and passed the morning helping with food preparation and cleaning. They dedicated half an hour to scripture study both day and night, and spent the second half of the day on schoolwork and studies. In addition to regular school subjects, the girls also learned Chinese. They loved drama and oratory and frequently recited poetry and performed plays for the home's frequent visitors. Donaldina's sewing instruction proved invaluable, and soon the girls made all of their own clothing, as well as the bed linens for the home. One of the older girls obtained a factory sewing job, which enabled her to earn enough money to return to China.[7]

Though the house valued industry, Donaldina knew the importance of play. She took the girls on outings in small groups so they had one-on-one time with her, and one or two girls always accompanied her on errands. She frequently planned outings to Golden Gate Park or the beach, where she waded into the surf with the children or let them bury her feet in the sand. On one occasion, Donaldina rode the ferry to Oakland with eight girls ranging in ages from five to twelve. One asked her, "Mama, how long 'til we get there?" A curious group of tourists looked at this unconventional family and inquired, "Pardon me, Madam. But are these little girls really yours?" Not feeling the need to explain to a stranger, Donaldina simply smiled and answered, "Indeed they are."[8]

In 1900, the new director resigned, and Donaldina officially stepped into the role, though little changed from the girls' perspective. Donaldina first learned to conduct rescue work from Margaret Culbertson, and she took to the challenge immediately, discovering an uncanny knack for finding human cargo, regardless of the lengths the underground network took to hide it. Donaldina credited God with the second sense she developed, moving aside wall panels and floor coverings to discover trapdoors, underground tunnels, and secret passageways. On one occasion, she rolled back linoleum flooring to reveal a trapdoor; beneath it, four girls shivered in a suspended box.[9] The media claimed she rescued 3,000 girls over the course of her career, though Donaldina herself shrugged and admitted she never kept track.

Over the years she served as home director, Donaldina gained the trust of local police and developed a complex network of Chinese informants. When a rescue call came in, she dropped anything else she was doing. Taking one of the older girls to act as translator, she plunged into the dungeons and alleyways of Chinatown with the first policeman she could find by her side. She acted immediately because if the slave owner received word she was coming, the captive would be whisked away to another hiding place.

In one of the most publicized raids that revealed the degree to which officials abetted criminal rings, Donaldina rescued a slave girl, Kum Qui, and rushed her home through a heckling crowd. A week later, a complicit policeman and Kum Qui's former owner appeared at the home with a warrant for the girl's arrest on falsified charges of larceny. Donaldina turned her over to the policeman's care, but then followed the group to Palo Alto, where Kum Qui was jailed; Donaldina shared her cell. During the night, the jailer opened the prison door to three men who overpowered Donaldina and dragged Kum Qui into a waiting buggy. When Donaldina tried to follow, the men flung her from the carriage into the street.

While Donaldina searched for help, the abductors whisked Kum Qui to a justice of the peace who agreed to hold impromptu court at 2:30 a.m. on a remote road. He found her guilty and demanded a fine of five dollars, which her abductors paid, thereby obtaining legal possession of her. Transporting Kum Qui swiftly to San Francisco, they forced her through a marriage ceremony with one of her abductors.

Meanwhile, as morning broke in Palo Alto, Donaldina notified the press as well as local authorities. As word of the scandal spread across the campus of Stanford University, an enraged mob of citizens and students descended on the jail where Kum Qui had been held. They marched with lanterns and torches, burning an effigy of the corrupt official and demanding arrests of those involved. Thanks to a tip from her network, Donaldina discovered the group at the San Francisco depot, and police took Kum Qui's abductors into custody. Palo Alto officials held a public meeting attended by thousands, where Donaldina calmly recited her story. Several in attendance commented on her grace and strength in spite of the circumstances, and the *San Francisco Chronicle* reported, "We admire the fearless, heroic, and womanly action of Miss Cameron in her efforts to prevent the abduction of her ward, which was accomplished under the guise of the law."[10]

The rescue of Kum Qui and similar cases brought Donaldina a

hard-earned measure of notoriety and fame, which drew prestigious visitors to the home. When President Theodore and Edith Roosevelt visited in 1901, they were entertained with speeches and plays, and left 920 Sacramento Street declaring the inhabitants, "The most charming little people they had ever met."[11]

The case of Kum Qui also brought greater awareness to the need for legal reform. Prior to the incident, Donaldina frequently broke the law by taking rescued girls into immediate custody, knowing the captives would disappear long before an official warrant could be issued. She was unofficially permitted to operate this way, and local police were instructed to "do whatever she tells you," assured that Donaldina's actions would be exonerated by any judge before whom she appeared. After the rescue of Kum Qui, however, Donaldina worked closely with her lawyer, Henry Monroe, to pass laws that gave a judge the right to place a rescued child with a temporary guardian: this essential reform was a breakthrough both for Donaldina's industry and the field of child law as a whole.[12]

This progress only strengthened the resentment of her enemies. As immigration restrictions tightened, the street price of Chinese females soared. The "tongs"[13] viewed Donaldina as one of the main obstacles in their way to wealth and determined to be rid of her. One day Donaldina received an anonymous call, tipping her off regarding a girl in need of rescue. When Donaldina arrived at the described location, she found an effigy of herself dangling from the ceiling with a dagger thrust through its heart. Though shaken by the experience, she refused to take counsel from the tong's threats. Her work had to continue.[14]

As girls grew into women in the mission home, some returned to China, while others left to pursue education as doctors, nurses, and teachers. Yoke Yeen became the first Chinese woman to graduate from Stanford University, and Jade Jeong completed Women's

Medical College in Philadelphia. Hopeful suitors called upon the house; if they were honorable men able to support a family, their courtship was welcome, though Donaldina encouraged her wards to marry for love. Weddings became frequent events in the mission home, which was decorated with vines, white roses, dahlias, and chrysanthemums for the occasions. The cook prepared wedding cake and traditional Chinese sweets. In the Chinese custom, brides traditionally wore red, but Donaldina encouraged her "daughters" to wear white, emphasizing that their troubled pasts lay behind them, and a new life ahead.[15] Playing the role of both father and mother, Lo Mo walked brides to the altar to strains of the wedding march.

Sometimes the girls teased Donaldina about her own romantic prospects. Donaldina was quite young when she first arrived at the mission home and assumed that eventually she would marry. At the age of thirty-five, she fell in love with a charming and entertaining football player, but the romance did not last, and though Donaldina was disappointed by the outcome, she viewed it as God's will.

After Donaldina had run the home for several years, everyone agreed that she had earned an extended rest. She began by visiting extended family in Scotland, the fulfillment of a lifelong dream. After that, she went on to China, where Donaldina spent the next three months speaking with officials and merchants about the slave trade, begging for assistance to stop the trans-Pacific trafficking. She spent the majority of time in Kwantung (Canton) province, as most of her girls came from this region, but she also marveled at the beauty of Shanghai, where she continued speaking out at schools, churches, and homes, pleading with people to stop the slave trade. Donaldina spoke with the help of an interpreter. In spite of substantial effort, she was never able to learn the Chinese language fluently, a fact Donaldina blamed on her family's notorious tone deafness, which made it impossible to pick up the language's inflections and intonations. At the end of her trip, sixty exuberant girls and young women welcomed her home.

Donaldina's loving and generous heart won over all who knew her, but it sometimes got her into trouble for bending rules. Though the house didn't officially accept babies, Donaldina couldn't bear to turn them away. She was known to say, "Who can fathom the possibilities concealed in so small a form?"[16] There were three babies in the house on the fateful morning of April 18, 1906, when Donaldina fell from her bed at 5:13 a.m., tossed by an intense swaying of the ground beneath her.

She would later describe the catastrophic earthquake as "the never-to-be-forgotten moments the solid earth took on the motions of an angry ocean while chimneys crashed onto our roof, while plaster and ornaments strewed the floors."[17] Shrieks sounded throughout the house. Older girls helped soothe the little ones as Donaldina surveyed the damage. When the swaying building came to a stop, it was damaged, but miraculously still standing, though many "walls of brick and wood around caved and crumbled." Donaldina instructed the girls to dress and gather in the dining room for a hasty breakfast of bread sent by a nearby bakery. They sang a hymn and repeated the Twenty-third Psalm, "with more feeling . . . than ever before."[18]

While finishing breakfast, an aftershock rocked the house, and a more ominous threat became clear. From the top-story windows, Donaldina watched plumes of smoke rise from around the city as dark clouds billowed into the sky. Shouts of "Fire!" rang out as the streets quickly filled with fleeing refugees. Knowing the tongs would be eager to recapture her charges, Donaldina felt it would be far too dangerous to move the household once it was dark, so she decided to evacuate immediately to a nearby Presbyterian church. All available hands gathered all food, bedding, and clothing that could be carried.

Three small babies, including one less than a month old, with her newly rescued mother, made the travel even more complicated.

The group found shelter in the Presbyterian church, but in the middle of the night, Donaldina awoke in the darkness, her mind upon the house at 920. In their haste to leave, she had forgotten the records of her daughters' identities as well as the paperwork granting her guardianship. If the paperwork was destroyed by fire, her enemies would be sure to guess she no longer had documentation. If they returned to court, she might lose some of the girls. Donaldina awoke no one but arose in the dark, trusting God's protection as she fled back through the streets now abandoned by all except looters and soldiers. A guard stopped her in front of a blockaded street, but Donaldina charmed and convinced the officer to allow her passage.

The outline of the mission home stood silhouetted against flames burning only a few blocks away. As she climbed up the front steps, a soldier shouted at her to halt. Donaldina's eyes burned with a fury to match the inferno behind her. "This is the Mission Home for rescued slave girls. I am its director. I must get my girls' records to protect them." The soldier raised his gun and said, "I have orders to shoot anyone who tries to enter a building." "Shoot then!" Donaldina replied, and she ducked inside. Rushing to her office, Donaldina gathered up the precious reports and court orders.

An explosion rocked the building and glass shattered to the floor. "Come out!" yelled the guard who had followed her. "They are dynamiting in the next block."[19] Donaldina grabbed the necessary files and looked back one last time at the home already beginning to glow in the light of flame. As the guard escorted her back up the hill, ash and cinders swirled through the night sky around them. With the important paperwork safe in her arms, Donaldina returned to her sleeping daughters.

By dawn, fire threatened the church as well, and it became

clear that the group would need to move again. A new refuge, this time a barn, was identified, but its distant location meant the girls would have to walk four long miles. To prepare for the journey, they strapped babies onto the older girls' backs and used broom handles to bundle the bedding and clothes. Even five-year-old Hung Mooie carried two dozen eggs, encouraged by the promise she would be able to eat them. Donaldina reported, "As tears would not avail (the hour for weeping had not yet come), laughter was the tonic which stimulated that weary, unwashed, and uncombed procession on the long tramp through stifling, crowded streets . . . where fires of yesterday still smoldered."[20] The girls took refuge in the barn before moving to a nearby church until their home could be rebuilt, using the same bricks that had been warped and shaped by the fire.

Romance visited Donaldina's life once more the year she turned forty. A handsome missionary-minded man named Nathaniel Tooker had long aided her efforts, and Donaldina considered his daughters close friends. When she was invited to speak at an annual meeting of the Synod of California, Utah, and Nevada, Donaldina called upon her audience to help change laws at the root of the slave trade. She said, "Let us set in motion a vast machine to abolish prejudice and enforce laws for the well-being of the Chinese."[21] The speech was well-received by the Tookers and her supporters, but others in the audience refused to applaud; she later learned they felt a woman had no business offering advice on political issues. Nathaniel, however, was charmed. A few weeks later, when Donaldina visited New York, he proposed. She accepted and returned to San Francisco, planning to conclude her work and join him in the East. In July, only a few short months before their wedding date, Donaldina received an urgent telegram from Nathaniel's daughter. "Lean hard and take courage," it said. "Father died today."[22] Devastated by this turn of events, Donaldina traveled to Hawaii with her beloved niece. After several months of healing, Donaldina returned to 920 Sacramento Street determined not to consider marriage again. She would devote the remainder of her life to the work of the mission home.

For twenty-five more years, Donaldina served as director. When the home became too crowded, she oversaw construction of a separate home for the smallest children. She persuaded a local pastor to begin a similar home for boys, fulfilling a need that had long weighed on her heart. She continued raids and rescues, traveling up and down the West Coast from Seattle to Los Angeles in search of trafficked women. From around the world, letters returned to her, bringing word from beloved daughters. "My Much Loved Mother," one began. "It is now some months since I left you, but even when I sleep I do not forget you."[23]

In support of the war effort during World War I, Donaldina sent her older girls to work in fruit orchards. Her growing fame led to an invitation to meet with President Woodrow Wilson, but she had to cancel the meeting at the last minute when she received news that a captive in Chicago needed recovery. To Donaldina, a girl in need was more important than the president of the United States. Her devotion was amply returned, and Tien, the rebellious child who once rebuffed Lo Mo's friendship, returned in adulthood to work as Donaldina's assistant.

Due in part to Donaldina's work at the home, prostitution in the city slowly declined. However, one ring of criminals, run by the wealthy merchant Wong See Duck, eluded prosecution. In 1935, a desperate girl knocked on the door of 920, begging for help. Jeung Gwai Ying[24] had been lured from her financially desperate family in Hong Kong by the promise of a waitressing job in San Francisco. Once through immigration, however, she had been sold to Wong See Duck, who threatened her with violence if she did not engage in prostitution. Desperate to escape, she heard of Donaldina's work while having her hair done a few blocks from the mission home. Leaving the appointment before her captors returned, she asked a young boy for directions to the mission home. Jeung Gwai Ying and three others in Donaldina's care had all endured similar treatment by the powerful Wong See Duck.

Donaldina knew that these girls had the ability to convict the tong leader, if they were willing to testify, an excruciating experience considering the abuse they had faced. But Jeung Gwai Ying particularly wanted to testify, to see her captors receive the justice they deserved.

During the first trial, however, the pressure from aggressive cross-examination and complicit witnesses proved too much. Jeung Gwai dropped her face to her hands and couldn't continue. The accused walked free. Three days after the traumatic event, however, Wong So was brought to the house; she also identified Wong See Duck as her captor. Now with three witnesses against him, they returned to trial. In spite of multiple death threats, Donaldina successfully coached the girls through the process of testifying and thus successfully broke one of the most pernicious trafficking rings in the city.

Donaldina's assistant wrote of the event, "This decision will have a far-reaching effect. Girls may hear of it and learn that they can run away. The slave owners will be frightened and deterred."[25] When the powerful and wealthy Wong See Duck and several of his cronies were jailed, fined, and deported due to Lo Mo and her daughters' testimonies, the Chinatown slave trade was essentially dismantled. The event caused great celebration at number 920.

Though Donaldina officially retired as director at age sixty-five, she remained involved in the work for the rest of her life. At age seventy, she bought a home with two of her older sisters, and the three became known for their hospitality and generosity. Reflecting on her long career, she jokingly confided, "I am glad I did not settle for matrimony. . . . If I had my life to live over again I'd do it the same way. Only I'd be better prepared."[26] By age eighty-one, she was the only Cameron sister remaining, and when Tien retired, Donaldina invited her to live next door. Donaldina remained in continual contact with the new director Lorna Logan, traveling regularly to the mission home, which they renamed the Donaldina Cameron House in her honor. During one such visit, she entertained the children with stories of daring escapes and the inspiring accomplishments of Tien and her predecessors. As her story drew to a close, she asked her eager young listeners: "What are you going to do with *your* life?"[27]

❦

It is a question that echoes through a century and a half of passing years. Trying to fit Donaldina's ninety-eight years into these short pages is an exercise in frustration; I've captured only a snapshot of her adventures, mishaps, and triumphs. Rarely does one find a life as devoted to a single cause as hers. Her capacity to share love and joy with those around her seemingly knew no bounds. Certainly, she could be a stern disciplinarian, and at times pushed herself to the brink of mental and emotional breakdowns. More than a century later, some have criticized the conversion of her girls to Christianity and view her as one more white woman intent on saving a "less fortunate" race.

But I do not think these criticisms hold much water when the details of her life are closely scrutinized. Like Tien, who was eventually won over by Lo Mo's sincerity and love, it's impossible to read Donaldina's writings and miss the profound respect she had for Chinese culture, evidenced by the fact that her girls spoke Chinese, retained many traditions, and often returned to their homeland. The girls she rescued were not her professional responsibilities—they were her family, and she treated them quite literally as her daughters.

Records indicate that, though influenced by prevailing notions of white superiority, Donaldina did not force the conversion of her girls. The Christian environment of the home was an extension of Donaldina's faith: the sustaining, driving force of her own life. She felt guided by God in all her work, and even her enemies acknowledged that her ability to discover their secret lairs was nothing short of supernatural.

To me, Donaldina's question "What are you going to do with *your* life?" remains both poignant and compelling. There are multitudes who suffer in modern variations of slavery; sex trafficking is no longer confined to one race, but it is estimated that 20.9 million victims of human trafficking globally[28] still suffer from this horrific reality, with hundreds of thousands in the United States alone. Those who are trafficked, either for labor or sex, live at the shadowed margins of society, and they are within our power to help. Beyond the bonds of physical slavery, many more are trapped by the twin shackles of poverty and isolation. Regardless of our religious persuasion, Donaldina's life reminds us to fill this world with love. As she once wrote in a director's report, "Have not we been sent to bind up the broken-hearted, to proclaim liberty to the captives and the opening of the prison to them that are bound? . . . With simple faithfulness, therefore, let us go forward looking to God for our pattern, then weave it into human life: thus will the world become better."[29]

FURTHER READING

Dorothy Gray, *Women of the West* (Millbrae, CA: Les Femmes Publishing, 1976).

Gloria G. Harris and Hannah S. Cohen, *Women Trailblazers of California: Pioneers to the Present* (Charleston, SC: History Press, 2012).

Mildred Crowl Martin, *Chinatown's Angry Angel: The Story of Donaldina Cameron* (Palo Alto, CA: Pacific Books, 1977).

Kristin and Kathryn Wong, *Fierce Compassion: The Life of Abolitionist Donaldina Cameron* (Saline, MI: New Earth Enterprises, 2012).

NOTES

1. Mildred Crowl Martin, *Chinatown's Angry Angel: The Story of Donaldina Cameron* (Palo Alto, CA: Pacific Books, 1977), 271.

2. Dorothy Gray, *Women of the West* (Millbrae, CA: Les Femmes Publishing, 1976), 69.

3. Martin, *Chinatown's Angry Angel*, 35.

4. Gloria G. Harris and Hannah S. Cohen, *Women Trailblazers of California: Pioneers to the Present* (Charleston, SC: History Press, 2012), 63.

5. Ibid.

6. Martin, *Chinatown's Angry Angel*, 65.

7. Ibid., 63.

8. Ibid., 60.

9. Ibid., 138.

10. Ibid., 56.

11. Ibid., 62.

12. Gray, *Women of the West*, 72.

13. The term *tongs* applies to any Chinese business coalition; the term is frequently associated with criminal activity but not exclusively so.

14. Martin, *Chinatown's Angry Angel*, 54.

15. In the Victorian and post-Victorian era of Donaldina's work, this stance on female sexuality was actually very forward thinking. Many of her contemporaries viewed any single female who had engaged in sex, willingly or not, to be soiled and damaged goods, unworthy of wearing a white wedding gown. Though some critics have argued that Donaldina should have maintained the Chinese tradition, her point was one that was relevant and directed toward contemporary observers.

16. Martin, *Chinatown's Angry Angel*, 172.

17. http://www.sfmuseum.net/1906/ew15.html.

18. Ibid.

19. Martin, *Chinatown's Angry Angel*, 105.

20. http://www.sfmuseum.net/1906/ew15.html.

21. Martin, *Chinatown's Angry Angel*, 142.

22. Ibid., 152.

23. Ibid., 78.

24. Because the Chinese names in this chapter are transliterated from a language that does not use the Latin alphabet, spellings are approximate and appear in several different ways. Wong See Duck appears in some sources as Wong She Duck, while Jeung Gwai Ying appears as Kwai Ying.

25. Martin, *Chinatown's Angry Angel*, 261.

26. Ibid., 271.

27. Ibid., 281.

28. See http://www.ilo.org/global/about-the-ilo/newsroom/news/WCMS_182109/lang—en/index.htm.

29. Martin, *Chinatown's Angry Angel*, 7.

CHAPTER 11

CHARLEY PARKHURST
MOST CELEBRATED STAGECOACH DRIVER IN THE WEST

Born: 1812, Sharon, Vermont
Died: December 29, 1879, Watsonville, California

"That a young woman should assume man's attire and, friendless and alone, . . . achieve distinction in an occupation above all professions calling for the best physical qualities of nerve, courage, coolness, and endurance . . . seems almost fabulous."[1]

Some frontier lives raise more questions than they can possibly answer as facts entwine with folklore, blending over time into a knot of fables impossible to untangle. Such is the life of Charley Parkhurst, notorious in her day as one of the most celebrated stagecoach drivers in the West. Her fame passed into the stuff of legends when it was discovered at her death that she was not, in fact, born male, as most people had assumed during her adult life.

There are a multitude of reasons why a woman on the frontier might assume a male identity. Certainly "unprotected" females were limited in opportunities for education and careers, and they were often vulnerable to unwanted sexual advances. The confined gender roles of the 1800s prescribed a narrow set of suitable behaviors; any woman who dared to ignore traditions left herself open to criticism and scorn. Two hundred years later, it's impossible to determine the reasons that motivated Charley's decision to pass as a male, but one thing is certain: she thrived in the identity she constructed for herself.

Originally named Charlotte Parkhurst, she was born in New Hampshire in 1812. Little is known about her early life, but we do know that her mother passed away when Charlotte was still very young. Like many children left alone in the world, Charlotte and her sister were sent to an orphanage in Massachusetts after their mother's death. The orphanages of the 1800s were daunting institutions—highly regimented systems where corporal punishment was the norm. Many reports indicate that orphans faced hunger, abuse, and overwork. At the age of twelve, Charlotte stole a boy's outfit and ran away from the orphanage.

Sometime later, a stable owner discovered Charlotte hiding in his barn in Worcester, Massachusetts. Startled by the unknown child, Ebenezer Balch initially told "him" to leave, but reconsidered when he noticed that the horses responded to the "lad" unusually well. So instead of evicting the skinny stowaway, Ebenezer put Charlotte—now known as Charley—to work cleaning stables and caring for his animals. Charley loved to watch the stagecoach drivers and showed interest in all aspects of horsemanship. Ebenezer trained her to drive, first one horse, then two, then a set of four, and finally a team of six—a skill that was fairly rare and required a great deal of dexterity.[2] By the time she was twenty, Charley was known as one of the best drivers on the East Coast. People began requesting her by name, and some loyal customers would ride only if Charley handled the reins.

Charley moved from Massachusetts to Rhode Island with Balch, then on to Iowa. Legend has it that when Charley applied for a job with the Overland Stage Line, several men vied to fill the position. The owner, Ben Holiday, asked, "How close could you allow the stage to get to a thousand-foot drop and be sure the passengers would be safe?" One driver called out, "Two feet!" Another, "Five inches!" One said he could make it with half the tire hanging over the edge. Charley turned to walk away and called back, "I'd stay as far away from the edge of that cliff as the hubs would let me." "You are just the man I want!" called Holiday, and he offered Charley the job.

In the late 1840s, gold fever spread around the country, and many of Charley's colleagues headed to California. Now in her late thirties, she decided to join the exodus. She sailed from Boston to Panama, then crossed overland to pick up a ship on the Pacific side. In Panama, Charley told John Morton, the owner of a shipping company: "I aim to be the best damn driver in California."[3] Morton must have believed Charley because he offered her a job.

In the gold rush days of California, stagecoach drivers were among the most respected, important members in the community. They rode at the front of the stage, subject to every kind of weather—facing storms, hazardous conditions, bandits, and potentially hostile Indians. Stagecoaches comprised the arteries and blood flow of the West: carrying breaking news, transporting valuables, and providing the main form of transportation for passengers as well. The stages rattled over "roads," still wild and unbroken, winding through mountain passes alongside sheer drops of thousands of feet. Stages often encountered flash floods, fallen logs, wild animals, and holdups. It was a dangerous job, and handlers rode armed and ready for conflict. Since stages were not equipped with horns, drivers used their fingers to blast a shrill warning whistle to oncoming traffic before rounding blind corners.[4]

Soon after Charley's arrival in California during the middle of a run, a horse threw a shoe; Charley knelt to replace it when the animal kicked her in the eye. She lost the use of that eye and began wearing a patch, but she refused to allow injury to impact her driving. On a previous occasion she rolled an empty stage and "busted in" her sides, but refused to see a doctor. After the eye injury, people began calling her "One-Eyed Charley," just one of many nicknames given to the soon famous driver. Some folks dubbed her "Six Horse Charley" because of her ability to handle a large team. Another popular nickname for stagecoach drivers was "jehu" after the Biblical passage, "and the driving is like the driving of Jehu the son of Nimshi; for he driveth furiously" (2 Kings 9:20). A true jehu, Charley indeed drove furiously.

But the biggest compliment of all came from the people who called her a "whip," a term applied to the best and fastest drivers. The term came from the custom-made leather horsewhip that was every driver's prized possession. When driving a team of six, Charley held three pairs of reins in her left hand; she used her right to apply the friction brake and whip as needed. With her whip, Charley could snap a cigar out of a fellow's mouth at fifteen paces.[5] This precision extended to her driving as well, and reportedly she could drive over a half-dollar left lying in the road with both her front and back wheels.

Charley's driving adventures in the Wild West grew to mythical proportions. On one occasion, a heavy storm left a river near Modesto, California, swollen and spilling over its bounds. Partway across the bridge, Charley felt the wooden structure breaking to pieces beneath her stage. Speeding the horses forward, Charley raced for solid ground as the bridge collapsed into the river just behind her. Thanks to lightning-fast reflexes, her passengers remained safe. In fact, Charley never injured a passenger, though there were a few close calls, including the time an animal startled Charley's horses, and they veered off the road. Tossed right off the driver's seat, Charley somehow managed to hold on to the reins while being dragged along, until she could finally stop the spooked horses. When the crazy, off-road ride came to an end, the grateful passengers collected twenty dollars to tip their gutsy driver.

In the early 1850s, Charley had a run-in with the notorious bandit Sugarfoot, so called due to the sugar sacks he wore on his feet in order to obscure his tracks. In their first encounter, Sugarfoot's gang took Charley by surprise, holding her at gunpoint as they forced her to throw down the strongbox containing all the coach's valuables. Even as she tossed it down, Charley promised the thieves that she would "break even with them."[6] She swore she would never be robbed again, and, true to her word, the next time Sugarfoot held up Charley's coach, Charley raised her shotgun before the outlaw had time to blink. She shot and mortally wounded Sugarfoot, then applied her whip to the frightened team—driving off without further interruption.

Two other bandits dared attempt a robbery of Charley's stage. One aimed a gun at Charley and ordered her to put her hands in the air, a command Charley acknowledged only with the crack of her whip across the outlaw's eyes; the stage rolled on. On another occasion, a would-be robber stood in the middle of the road with his gun leveled at the oncoming coach. In a bold move, Charley charged the man, pulling back hard on the reins so the horses reared into the air directly over the bandit. As the villain scrambled for safety, the stagecoach continued down the road at a fast gallop.[7] After these incidents, word spread through the community, and bandits let Charley's coach roll past in peace. The *San Francisco Morning Call* proclaimed her to be "the most dexterous and celebrated of the California drivers . . . and it was an honor to be striven for to occupy the spare end of the driver's seat when the fearless Charley Parkhurst held the reins of a four- or six-in-hand."[8]

Charley frequently covered sixty miles in a day over rough and muddy roads, sometimes even picking up a second shift, which meant driving back over the same route through the night. She covered the line from Oakland to San Jose and was the "boss of the road" between San Juan and Santa Cruz,[9] working for several companies, including Wells Fargo. In addition to her skill as a whip, she gained a reputation as a talented horse doctor, and some even called her a horse whisperer. *Vaqueros* (Spanish cowboys) from around the state brought their sick horses to Charley for treatment and advice.

In physical appearance, she was described as being short, thin, and wiry, with a high-pitched voice. Some characteristics that might have given away Charley's gender were dismissed as quirks. For instance, she wore gloves constantly, even at meals, and never grew facial hair. She was a confirmed "bachelor," and requested a change to her Placerville route to avoid female "Mormons who were of 'a marrying disposition.'"[10] At night, she often bedded down with the horses in the stable. When asked why, she replied, "I get along better with horses than folks."[11] However, one of Charley's companions claimed she "out-swore, out-drank, and out-chewed even the Monterey whalers." Though she remained a bit of an enigma, the famous driver was known for her kind heart; she always kept a piece of candy in her pocket to give to children.

But a body—even one as tough as Charley's—cannot endure the rigors of stage driving forever. After nearly thirty years of driving, Charley gave up the profession in her fifties, partly due to rheumatism,[12] a common complaint among drivers. Additionally, as railroads arrived in the West, the age of the stagecoach drew to a close. After retirement, Charley settled outside Watsonville, California, and tried her hand at a variety of jobs, including running a stage shop, working as a lumberman, cattle ranching, saloon keeping, and chicken farming. She took a business partner named Frank Woodward, and the two joined the Odd Fellows Association, an organization devoted to charitable causes. Her kindness to the community took many forms. Once when a widow and her daughter were about to lose their home to foreclosure, Charley bought the place and graciously returned it to her friends. For a time, the town gossips conjectured that Charley might begin a romance with the daughter, but, not surprisingly, nothing developed.

In the 1860s, Charley stayed with the Clark family while engaged in logging work. According to family reports, Charley returned home drunk one night and Mrs. Clark asked her seventeen-year-old son to help Charley to bed. The boy returned exclaiming, "Maw, Charley ain't no man, he's a woman."[13] The story went unreported until after Charley's death, so the validity is difficult to verify—but the tale is just one more place where Charley's life blends into folklore.

Charley registered to vote in 1868, forty-three years before California passed women's suffrage, and fifty-two years before the Nineteenth Amendment gave all white United States women the right to engage in the democratic process. Records aren't conclusive about whether or not she cast a ballot in the presidential election that year, but if she did, she was the first woman to do so.

Charley's chronic chewing tobacco habit eventually caught up with her, and in her final days, she suffered from cancer of the tongue. In a little cabin outside of Watsonville, she treated her illness with horse remedies, saying, "If it's good enough fer me horses, it's good enough fer me."[14] Local doctors recommended procedures that might have prolonged her life, but Charley refused. In her last days, she was assisted by friends and neighbors, and in her will, she left six hundred dollars to twelve-year-old George Harmon, a neighbor boy who had cared for her. Charley instructed her friends that she wanted to be buried in her grubby everyday clothes, but these instructions were not followed. Friends insisted on washing and preparing the body, and when they did so, they were shocked to discover that their acclaimed associate was, in fact, a woman.

The doctor called in to confirm the discovery stated, after further examination, that at some point Charley had given birth; a crimson dress and pair of baby shoes discovered in Charley's tin chest seemed to corroborate the claim. When someone told business partner Frank Woodward the news, he was so upset he "didn't stop swearing for three days!"[15] Newspapers around the country echoed the shock of the community in California. The *New York Times* conjectured: "That a young woman should assume man's attire and, friendless and alone, . . . achieve distinction in an occupation above all professions calling for the best physical qualities of nerve, courage, coolness, and endurance, and that she should add to them the almost romantic personal bravery that enables one to fight one's way through the ambush of an enemy, seems almost fabulous."[16]

The Odd Fellows Association handled the shock more graciously than others. In spite of the fact that they did not allow female members at the time, they still buried Charley with full lodge honors because she had been so respected by her peers.[17] Laid to rest in the Odd Fellows Cemetery, the scandal must have given Charley's contemporaries engaged in hot debates over women's rights a great deal to think about. Indeed, the *Providence Journal* observed, "The only people who have any occasion to be disturbed by the career of Charley are the gentlemen who have so much to say about 'women's sphere' and the 'weaker vessel.'"[18] Meanwhile, her obituary in the *Santa Cruz Sentinel* concluded, "Who shall no longer say that a woman can not labor and vote like a man?"[19]

❧

Though subsequent generations have come and gone, Charley's story still raises more questions than it provides answers. While her decisions appear to have been motivated, in part, by a challenging set of childhood circumstances and an innate talent for a profession barred to her gender, her feelings about the choice she made are lost in the mists of time. Charley's story leaves me wondering what might have happened if she had attempted to be open about her gender and still pursue her passion. Would she have found employment? Would she have felt free to approach her life with the same grit and passion? If not, then what is it that holds us back from living the lives we deeply desire? Is it a combination of society's expectations mingled with our own fears? Ironically, by hiding aspects of her identity, Charley became free to express herself more fully, to explore talents and interests that her society was not ready to accept in a woman. Though we've made immense amounts of progress in some areas (women's suffrage comes to mind), judgments from a broader culture about what is acceptable can still be heavy burdens, weighing us down in a journey toward a fuller acceptance of ourselves.

If Charley did bear a child, at some point *someone* else was aware she was female. Perhaps to achieve her own goals, she showed a broader society what it wanted to see—a male whip as hardened as the rocky trail over which he drove his coach. But for someone worthy of her secret, Charley was willing to share her identity as a woman as well. This is pure conjecture, of course, and the circumstances under which she gave birth may have been far different from those I'm imagining. Regardless of the truth buried in the fragments of legend, Charley's story offers an invitation to consider what we choose to share and what we choose to withhold from others, the sacrifices we are willing to make to follow our dreams, and the example of a life lived right on the line between what society calls possible and impossible. Wherever she is now, I hope she is riding free, in all her strength and glory.

FURTHER READING

Sylvia Branzei (illustrations by Melissa Sweet), *Cowgirls: Rebel in a Dress* (New York: Running Press, 2011).

Mary Rodd Furbee, *Outrageous Women of the American Frontier* (New York: John Wiley & Sons, 2002).

Gloria G. Harris and Hannah S. Cohen, *Women Trailblazers of California: Pioneers to the Present* (Charleston, SC: History Press, 2012).

Fern J. Hill, *Charley's Choice: The Life and Times of Charley Parkhurst* (West Conshohocken, PA: Infinity Publishing, 2012).

Alton Pryor, *Fascinating Women in California History* (Roseville, CA: Stagecoach Publishing, 2011).

Ed Sams, *The Real Mountain Charley* (Ben Lomond, CA: Yellow Tulip Press, 1995).

NOTES

1. "Thirty Years in Disguise," correspondence of the *San Francisco Call,* carried in *New York Times,* 9 January 1880, accessed online at http://query.nytimes.com/mem/archive-free/pdf?res=9502E2D9 1131EE3ABC4153DFB766838B699FDE.

2. Gloria G. Harris and Hannah S. Cohen, *Women Trailblazers of California: Pioneers to the Present* (Charleston, SC: History Press, 2012), 23.

3. Alton Pryor, *Fascinating Women in California History* (Roseville, CA: Stagecoach Publishing, 2011), 87.

4. Mary Rodd Furbee, *Outrageous Women of the American Frontier* (New York: John Wiley & Sons, 2002), 65.

5. Robert San Souci, "Charley Parkhurst's Secret," *Faces Magazine* 24, no. 1 (2007): 42–45.

6. "Thirty Years in Disguise."

7. Craig MacDonald, *Cockeyed Charley Parkhurst: The West's Most Unusual Stagewhip* (N.p.: Filter Press, 1973), 14.

8. Ed Sams, *The Real Mountain Charley* (Ben Lomond, CA: Yellow Tulip Press, 1995), 27.

9. "Thirty Years in Disguise."

10. Sams, *Real Mountain Charley,* 9.

11. San Souci, "Charley Parkhurst's Secret," 42–45.

12. Rheumatism was a common complaint for older coach drivers. The word is no longer used by doctors today, but rheumatism was an inflammation of the joints and the term covers hundreds of identifiable conditions today, including rheumatoid arthritis and back and neck joint inflammation.

13. Pryor, *Fascinating Women,* 88.

14. Verla Kay, *Rough, Tough Charley* (Berkeley, CA: Tricycle Press, 2007), 32.

15. Ibid.

16. "Thirty Years in Disguise."

17. Kay, *Rough, Tough Charley,* 32.

18. MacDonald, *Cockeyed Charley Parkhurst,* 14.

19. *Santa Cruz Sentinel,* January 3, 1880.

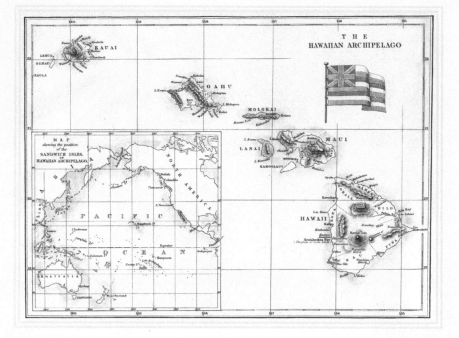

CHAPTER 12

MAKAOPIOPIO
THE SPIRIT OF ALOHA

Born: 1815, Ouli, Waimea, Hawaii
Death: September 15, 1889, Iosepa Colony, Utah

" . . . from the highlands of Waimea, to the brackish lowlands of Laie, up to the Rockies of Utah, and finally, to the desolation of Iosepa. Blessed by the voyages of her faith, we . . . pay honor and tribute to *tutu* Makaopiopio."[1]

On a brisk day in September, under a stainless blue sky, I drove west on I-80, passing the Great Salt Lake and piles of salt that have been culled from its waters. Near Tooele, I turned south, where Lone Rock and Horseshoe Springs once greeted the earliest pioneers to this valley. After following a road bordered by sagebrush and ranch lands, I saw a sign that marked the turnoff: Iosepa. In this unlikely place, nestled at the foothills of the Rocky Mountains, stands an empty gathering pavilion, a small graveyard, and, some distance away, a handful of crumbling foundations. Beyond these structures, the land sweeps away in an unbroken vista of prairie as far as the eyes can see. It is hard to believe that here a town once stood—a town once voted the "most progressive and picturesque in Utah."[2] Even more surprising is the knowledge that Iosepa was a Hawaiian colony where settlers spoke their native language and continued cultural practices, transplanted though they were to the desert. I have come seeking the grave of the first person to be buried in Iosepa, a woman named Makaopiopio, whose life began on the Big Island of Hawaii.

You will notice this chapter is quite different from others in this book, most notably because I cannot quote Makaopiopio directly. She was born at a time when Hawaiian was still largely an oral language; in fact, the dialect was not written at all prior to contact with white missionaries in the 1820s. Oral languages are fluid, and for that reason, her name appears in a few different variations, including Kamakaopiopio, a word that means "youthful eyes."[3] She would later assume a last name to fill out United States legal forms,[4] but in childhood, one name sufficed, and tribal genealogists preserved familial information by chanting lines of ancestry spanning many generations. Makaopiopio spoke Hawaiian her whole life and kept no written records, but her descendants may be found today in Utah; in Laie, Oahu; and on the island of Molokai. Though her voice has been lost to the intervening years, her memory lives on in her family members, in the close-knit community of Laie, and in annual Memorial Day celebrations that bring Iosepa's descendants together each spring for a traditional luau.[5]

In his book *Remembering Iosepa,* Matthew Kester points out that envisioning the arrival of whites in Polynesia as an extension of western expansion is an inherently western-centric notion. He argues that for far longer than whites were launching westward from the shores of California, Polynesians have been exploring outward from their islands. Voyaging canoes, or *va'a,* carried Polynesian explorers using navigational skills that predated the western world. Movement between islands, and to locations as far away as Alaska and New Zealand, were not unheard-of occurrences, so when Captain Cook arrived in 1778, the native Hawaiians welcomed him as a fellow sea voyager.[6] It is frequently forgotten that the flow of traffic went both ways, but Hawaiians and many other Polynesians joined whaling vessels or found other ways to emigrate to communities along the west coast of the United States. They could have little imagined the changes white explorers would bring to their islands, however.

Makaopiopio was born in 1815 in Ouli, Waimea, Hawaii. Raised in a village sheltered by groves of sandalwood trees in the Waimea Valley, her family and tribe practiced the religion of their ancestors. Kahunas, or priests, communicated with a pantheon of gods and goddesses expressed in the natural world. Pele, goddess of fire, ruled the volcanoes, and the *ohelo* berries that grew near volcanoes belonged to her. *Kapu,* or taboos, governed the actions of all, and breaking these strict rules was punishable by death. Sacred land containing waterfalls and volcanoes was reserved for the gods, along with their priests and priestesses. Another *kapu* strictly forbade men and women eating together; in fact, dietary laws prohibited women from eating certain foods such as coconut and pork, while other dishes were restricted to the *ali'i,* or ruling class, exclusively. Violation of the rules upset the *mana,* or power and life energy, of the whole community, causing suffering to all. Living in structures created from natural timbers and sweet-smelling *pili* grass, the ancient Hawaiians cultivated taro root, hunted wild pigs, and made leis from the blossoms of wild ginger and orchids. They enjoyed guava, *lilikoi,* mango, and mountain apples that grew in great abundance.

The arrival of white missionaries changed Hawaiian society in a number of ways. Perhaps most dramatically, these outsiders openly broke taboos, eating publicly with the opposite gender and climbing the sides of volcanoes to pick the *ohelo* berries—without negative consequences. The newcomers also brought unknown technologies about which the kahunas knew nothing, enhancing their perceived power of the outsiders. In the face of this evidence, many native Hawaiians began to doubt the veracity of traditional ways. Most devastating of all, white explorers brought illnesses including cholera, measles, and gonorrhea. Estimates place the population of

Hawaii before white contact at 250,000 to 1 million. By 1848, that native population had been decimated to around 88,000.[7]

Aided and represented by missionaries, the ruling Hawaiian elite formed trade agreements with the outside world, harvesting the sandalwood forests of Makaopiopio's youth and planting sugar cane and pineapple plantations. King Kamehameha, who unified the islands in 1810, recognized the potential for wealth that existed within the resources of the islands. The traditional Hawaiian view of land ownership taught that all land belonged to the gods; tribal leaders controlled certain areas, acting as guardians, but their members could use the land freely, taking from it what they needed in the form of fruit, plants, fish, and resources.[8] In 1845, Kamehameha III abolished this system and opened up land for purchase by foreigners. The United States quickly recognized the potential for labor and land, and over the course of the next few decades, the U.S. government eroded local power, overthrew the monarchy, and opened the islands for exploitation by foreign interests. By 1893, foreigners owned ninety percent of Hawaiian land. Native culture also came under attack, as Christian missionaries imposed their own traditions of dress and sexual monogamy, with inconsistent success. By the turn of the century, teachers conducted schools only in English, leading to a decline in the use of the Hawaiian language, and due to religious pressure, the government banned the practice of the hula.

Makaopiopio witnessed this dramatic evolution. Raised with two brothers and two sisters, she practiced traditional beliefs in her childhood, removed from outside influence. However, the Reverend Lorenzo Lyons, a Congregationalist minister, arrived in Waimea in 1832, and at some point, Makaopiopio converted to Christianity. She also gave birth to two daughters, Maria and Namahana. On April 20, 1842, Makaopiopio married a man named Kaohimaunu in a ceremony officiated by Father Lyons. The couple had four more children together: Mahunalii, Likabeka, Kailiwela, and Kahaole.

In 1850, missionaries from The Church of Jesus Christ of Latter-day Saints arrived in the islands. Initially they planned to proselytize only among the *haole* (white) inhabitants since none of the missionaries spoke Hawaiian, but they did not receive a warm welcome: already existing Christian groups protested new competition, sailors showed little interest, and the Hawaiian government refused to grant permission for the group to publicly gather.[9] Many of the missionaries became discouraged and decided to head back to the states. A few, however, including George Q. Cannon and Joseph F. Smith, decided to learn Hawaiian and preach to the native population. Surprisingly, they began to have success. Makaopiopio's husband was baptized in 1854, and records indicate that Makaopiopio joined him in 1862. The delay may have been due to opposition from her family or perhaps her own reluctance to convert again.

Makaopiopio and her husband purchased land near several other members of the Church in Laie, on the north shore of Oahu, where they worked on a Church-owned ranch, growing cotton, coffee, potatoes, and taro. A beautiful and vibrant community developed in the area, encompassed by lush green mountains on one side and the sparkling waves of Hukilau Bay on the other. Makaopiopio raised her children in Laie, sending them to a school established by Latter-day Saint missionaries.

About this time, one of the earliest LDS converts and most prominent Hawaiian leaders, Joseph Napela, visited Salt Lake City and returned to Laie with a positive report about the city. Though other Hawaiians hoped to visit Utah and possibly settle there, King Kamehameha IV watched the declining native population with alarm and did not want to lose more of his people to emigration, so he forbade the practice with few exceptions.

Makaopiopio's daughter Likabeka grew up with a young man named J.W. Kaulainamoku in Laie. In his teens, J.W. became close friends with one of the LDS missionaries from Utah, who invited J.W. to return to Utah with him at the conclusion of his mission. The King granted permission, and J.W. worked as a stonecutter on the Salt Lake Temple. Though Likabeka was a teenager when he left, a few years later, J.W. wrote requesting her hand in marriage, and Likabeka accepted. Joyfully, Makaopiopio and her husband planned to accompany their daughter to Utah for the wedding.

On the day they planned to sail, however, Makaopiopio and her husband arrived at the ship, only to learn that they had been denied passage. The reasons for the last-minute reversal are unclear, but it must have been discouraging for Makaopiopio to send her daughter off without the support of her parents. Fortunately, a close friend from Laie agreed to accompany Likabeka, which comforted Makaopiopio, though it hardly compensated for missing her daughter's wedding. Likabeka and J.W. were married in Salt Lake City in 1876.

The intervening years are ones we know little about, but at some point, Makaopiopio's daughter Maria joined her sister in Utah as well. Two years later, in 1879, Makaopiopio's husband passed away. Now widowed, Makaopiopio still longed to see Utah and visit her daughters, so she requested approval for the trip once more. New political leaders had reduced restrictions, and this time Makaopiopio received permission. Thrilled at the news, she departed nearly the same day.

A short five months after her husband's death, Makaopiopio, now in her sixties, sailed for San Francisco and traveled overland through the frigid Sierra Nevadas to Utah, arriving at Christmastime. Deeply grieving the loss of her husband, Makaopiopio's journey was motivated in part by a desire to reunite with her family and to visit the LDS temple.[10] She received a joyful welcome from her daughters and son-in-law after the family's long separation.

Seven years after Makaopiopio's arrival, her daughter Likabeka passed away from the dreaded disease leprosy. Though leprosy is curable today, it was a malady frequently associated with the Hawaiian islands, which only increased prejudice against Polynesian immigrants. Leprosy arrived in the islands in the 1830s, most certainly carried on ships from Europe, where it was fairly common; the prevalence of the disease led to the creation of the leper colony on the island of Molokai. The highly feared illness took years to manifest, and the method of contagion remained a mystery. Patients became disfigured with lumps and sores, many times beyond recognition. In the final stages, leprosy affects the eyes and extremities, causing severe pain and loss of sensation.

It is almost certain that Makaopiopio cared for her daughter as the disease progressed, which must have been both frightening, due to threat of contamination, and emotionally traumatic to witness the pain endured by her daughter. Ostracism from the surrounding community must have been difficult as well, and several local newspapers carried notice of Likabeka's progressing illness. After Likabeka's death, Makaopiopio stayed close to Maria, her grandchildren, and sons-in-law, as well as a network of extended family members and friends. Though four other children and several grandchildren still lived in the Hawaiian islands, after Likabeka's death, Makaopiopio remained in Utah.

Initially, LDS Hawaiian immigrants, including Likabeka and her husband, settled in West Valley in the Warm Springs area of Salt Lake City. Unfortunately, many of the Polynesian immigrants found adjusting to the broader community a challenge. Some experienced discrimination and prejudice from their white neighbors; others struggled to acclimate to the cold climate; and some found it difficult to gain employment. A part of local prejudice included fears about the danger of leprosy, which wasn't improved by Likabeka's death. Many people in the U.S. viewed leprosy as evidence of Polynesian sexual promiscuity, only amplifying misunderstanding and prejudice between the cultures.[11] Concerned about the community, religious leaders broached the possibility of starting a separate Hawaiian colony, like many of the other LDS satellite colonies established around the western United States and Canada.[12] The Hawaiian community responded positively, and they chose leaders, including J.W., to identify possible sites.[13] The committee compared a few different areas and decided on ranch land south of Tooele. In 1889, the LDS Church purchased 1,920 acres, and the Hawaiian Saints named their settlement Iosepa, which is Hawaiian for *Joseph*, in honor of Joseph F. Smith, their beloved missionary.

After months of preparation, these colonists traveled together to Garfield by train, then by wagon to Grantsville, where they spent the night, journeying south the next morning to the site of Iosepa.[14] J.W. built one of the first homes, separated from the rest of the community because Makaopiopio had now become ill with the same disease that had taken her daughter. Over time, the Hawaiian Saints would build houses, a general store, a school, a chapel, fire hydrants, and an irrigation system. They cultivated crops, planted trees, raised livestock, and even experimented with growing seaweed.[15] Though they often adopted new practices, many of the traditional ways remained. Records note the marketing of flower leis and poi bowls,[16] and Hawaiian remained the dominant language, though English was commonly spoken as well. Settlers created their own currency usable at the town store, and nearly all contemporary sources comment on the beauty of streets lined with poplar trees and yellow rose bushes.[17]

Makaopiopio, however, would not live to see these developments. Three weeks after her arrival, she succumbed to leprosy, becoming the first settler to die in Iosepa colony. Her death necessitated the choosing of a burial site, and community members selected a secluded area to serve as a graveyard. Here she was laid to rest, mourned by family and friends both nearby and an ocean away. Though her gravesite was marked, the headstone may have been made from wood or other delicate material. A few years later, a brush fire destroyed many of the markers in the cemetery, and today the exact location of her grave remains unknown. J.W. would also eventually be buried there.

The Iosepa colony would continue for another twenty-eight years. At its height, the land included a productive 5,000-acre ranch and a thriving town. In 1894, the settlement reported raising 14,000 bushels of grain, 1,850 bushels of wheat, and 1,650 bushels of oats.[18] The colony continued until Joseph F. Smith announced a temple would be built in Laie, at which time a few families withdrew to Salt Lake City, while most chose to return to the islands. Returning pioneers built homes on a street in Laie designated in their honor— to this day it is named Iosepa Street. The buildings and cultivation efforts in Iosepa, Utah, crumbled with passing years and returned to the earth. At this time, you can find remaining brick foundations and the cemetery with a memorial to the Hawaiian settlers. A separate monument honors Makaopiopio, the first one laid to rest there.[19]

Today, many from the continental United States are drawn to the Hawaiian Islands by their beauty, exquisite climate, and string of pristine beaches. Few understand the complicated history between the native Hawaiian population and the U.S. government, and land policies that left a small fraction of property in control of native people—but visitors may notice signs along the highways protesting continued exploitation. The Hawaiian culture, however, has remained strong. Native population is currently on the rise, paralleled by a profound interest in preserving Hawaiian language and culture.

Who could have predicted that this woman, born in the valley of Waimea, would someday find her way to the remote settlement of Iosepa, Utah? Without Makaopiopio's direct words, it is impossible to know how she felt about the events that unfolded around her. Without them, it is nearly impossible to reconstruct her identity, her voice, and her personality. But we do know what she did. Her actions remain, speaking on her behalf, conveying the power of identity through a lifetime of choices. She could have stopped at any point along her journey. She could have turned back after the loss of her daughter, but she did not. She chose to continue, first to Laie, then, in spite of the loss of her husband, to the vistas of Utah.

Her descendants in Laie explain that she is their beloved *tutu* (grandparent) and that part of her legacy was her choice to always go forward.[20] On the marker they erected in Iosepa, they wrote: "from the highlands of Waimea, to the brackish lowlands of Laie, up to the Rockies of Utah, and finally, to the desolation of Iosepa. Blessed by the voyages of her faith, we . . . pay honor and tribute to *tutu* Makaopiopio."[21]

Every Memorial Day, the ghost town of Iosepa comes to life as descendants of settlers from the islands and the valley gather for a luau celebration. With speeches, music, dance, and food, Iosepa lives again, evidence of the legacy that connects a ghost town on Utah's frontier with the islands of Hawaii. I wish Makaopiopio could see the integrated cultures paying tribute to her stalwart journey, to her ability to navigate enormous changes, and to the fascinating events underlying her life.

I first heard the story of Makaopiopio while teaching for a term at a university in Laie, Oahu. Though I had been raised on pioneer stories by my own grandmother, I had never heard of Iosepa. I was already enchanted with Laie, however. I rode my bike around Laie for the first few weeks, taking hundreds of pictures of plumeria blossoms, geckos, and turquoise waves arching in perfect crescendo. But most dazzling of all was this town where neighbors stopped to say hello, extend a dinner invitation, or ask for help with a neighborhood children's bake sale. When I forgot my wallet at the supermarket, a stranger behind me in line insisted on paying. As someone used to the reserve of mainland U.S. cities, the genuine warmth felt like something as antiquated as black-and-white movies (and just as lovely). I'd heard of *aloha,* a word that somehow simultaneously means *hello*, *good-bye*, and *love*—but I had never experienced it. Like falling in love changes a person, so does feeling aloha. Though I had been to Hawaii as a tourist, I realized I had missed the best part— the incredible feeling that comes from belonging to an intact, loving community—a place that connects individuals to part of a greater whole.

When I contacted Makaopiopio's descendants in Laie, Napua and Nalani welcomed me into their home and *ohana* (family), introducing the grandniece who was there for school, the grandson who had stopped by to say hello, and the son who was just leaving. Hawaiian families don't confine themselves to isolated spaces—they choose to live close in every way.

These two cousins, now in their seventies, were thrilled to help this *haole* writer learn about Makaopiopio, beginning with a lesson on how to pronounce her name. "Our *tutu* is so dear to us," they told me, speaking of the years in Laie and the settling of Iosepa, which they have visited on several occasions, with a familiarity so palpable the story might have been their own. As, in fact, it is.

I wish you, reader, could have sat next to me in that living room, adopted by these two loving Hawaiian aunties, marveling at the reminder that history is often more extraordinary than fiction—and that you cannot possibly ever hear all the stories there are to tell.

Napua concluded with gratitude for her ancestors. "They were a light to us, and now we are a light to those who come after—our children and grandchildren—the aloha and connection will continue on; long after we have left this earth, that light will remain."

Though Makaopiopio participated in some remarkable historical events, in many ways her life played out on a relatively small stage. Unlike other women in this book, she did not write pivotal new legislation or amass a fortune. She spent her life following an adopted faith, preserving culture, loving family, and building community in one place after another. She labored on the frontiers of two different lands—establishing a foundation of fellowship for those who would follow. To me, part of the significance of Makaopiopio's story is the reminder that there are many voices in history, and the dominant narrative is seldom the most interesting. Hers is one voice of a thousand perspectives we have lost, many in their entirety. Her story is a reminder of those other voices absent from this book—an invitation to find them when possible, and to feel the weight of the loss when it is not.

We can puzzle out the details of her life, but there is so much we do not know. Her experience is also a reminder that unless we want to live in a world of voices speaking on our behalf, we need to find a way to preserve and capture our experiences. An article published while Makaopiopio resided in Utah counseled readers: "If a man [or woman] keeps no diary, the path crumbles away behind him as his feet leave it; and days gone by are but little more than a blank, broken by a few distorted shadows. His [or her] life is all confined within the limits of today. Who does not know how imperfect a thing memory is?"[22] Thanks to Makaopiopio's descendants, we retain some of the events and choices of her life, but others have disappeared like a wave against the sands of Hukilau. Makaopiopio is a reminder to preserve your voice. Claim your memories. Take your pain and joy and experience living on this planet and translate them into black and white words—frozen in place, captured and sealed against time. But maybe she *did*, in fact, preserve her voice in the way that was most significant to her—through the strong connecting links of *aloha* she forged that continue today in those who love her. Perhaps her story is rather a call to love those around you with such fierceness that the world is changed for the better by your love.

FURTHER READING

Jacob Adler, *The Diaries of Walter Murray Gibson 1886–1887* (Honolulu: University of Hawaii Press, 1973).

Dennis H. Atkin, "Iosepa, A Utah Home for the Polynesians," http://scholarsarchive.byu.edu/cgi/viewcontent.cgi?article=1065&context=mphs.

Matthew Kester, *Remembering Iosepa: History, Place, and Religion in the American West* (New York: Oxford University Press, 2013).

Tom Wharton, "Remembering Iosepa and other determined Mormon Pioneers," *Salt Lake Tribune,* October 15, 2015.

NOTES

1. Kalama Ohana Family History, compiled by Theresa Maunahina Kalama Meyers Briggs, May 2002, 45.

2. Ouida Blanthorn, *A History of Tooele County* (Salt Lake City: Utah State Historical Society, 1998), 275–81.

3. Personal interview with Napua Baker and Nalani Fonoimoana, May 20, 2015, Laie, Oahu, Hawaii.

4. In some places her last name is listed as *Nui*. In others, it is *Kaohimaunu* (her husband's name).

5. Though the first Hawaiian Pioneer Day celebrations were held on the anniversary of the date the first settlers arrived, August 28, 1889, they are now held on Memorial Day for ease of scheduling.

6. Matthew Kester, *Remembering Iosepa: History, Place, and Religion in the American West* (New York: Oxford University Press, 2013), 1–27.

7. http://www.pewresearch.org/fact-tank/2015/04/06/native-hawaiian-population.

8. Jacob Adler and Robert M. Kamins, *The Fantastic Life of Walter Murray Gibson: Hawaii's Minister of Everything* (Honolulu: University of Hawaii Press, 1986), 77.

9. Kester, *Remembering Iosepa*, 51.

10. In LDS temples, ordinances are vicariously performed on behalf of those who have died, and Makaopiopio was vicariously married to her deceased husband for "time and all eternity."

11. Kester, *Remembering Iosepa*, 91.

12. For more on LDS settlements, see http://eom.byu.edu/index.php/colonization.

13. Some sources criticize the LDS Church for removing the Hawaiian Saints, saying leaders were motivated by prejudice and a desire to banish the Hawaiians to undesirable land. However, after reviewing the surviving documentation and journals, it is my opinion that these leaders, many of whom served missions in the islands and spoke Hawaiian fluently, genuinely cared about the Hawaiian settlers and were not motivated by prejudice (on the whole). The fact that they utilized Hawaiian leadership in all planning and implementation phases, coupled with a repeated pattern of establishing satellite communities, seems to support this conclusion.

   The end of the colony is a bit harder to explain, and while it is clear that many Hawaiian settlers wanted to return to the islands, it is just as clear that many did not. By that point, many Iosepa inhabitants had been born in the community and had never been to the islands at all. The discontinuation of a profitable and thriving community remains harder to understand or explain, though the LDS Church paid passage back to the islands and made sure returning settlers were welcomed.

14. Donald J. Rosenberg, "Concerning Iosepa, Utah," *Tooele Bulletin,* February 17, 1976 (LDS Church History Library).

15. Carol Edison, "South Sea Islanders in Utah," Iosepa Historical Association papers, 1908 (LDS Church History Library).

16. "Iosepa Branch, Utah Relief Society Minutes and Records, 1909–1912," October 13, 1910 (LDS Church History Library), 61.

17. Dennis H. Atkin, "Utah's Iosepa: Polynesian Beauty in the Desert" (Hilo, HI: Mormon Pacific Historical Society).

18. Rosenberg, "Concerning Iosepa." Rosenberg said he derived his articles from Dennis Atkin's work as well as interviews with Helen Hoopiiania and Alf Callister, former residents of Iosepa.

19. Some sources mistakenly suggest that Makaopiopio is not buried at the cemetery in Iosepa. However, the cemetery records specifically state she was the first to be buried there. Her great-great-granddaughters Napua Baker and Nalani Fonoimoana in Laie confirmed this, but clarified that the exact spot within the graveyard itself is unknown. Most likely her grave marker was made quickly and from less durable materials, causing it to erode over time. The cemetery records also indicate that many of the original wooden grave markers were burned by a brush fire in the early years of the settlement; hers may have been among them (see "Iosepa Cemetery, Burial Grounds of the Golden People from Hawaii," LDS Family History Library).

20. Personal interview with Napua Baker and Nalani Fonoimoana, May 20, 2015, Laie, Oahu, Hawaii.

21. Kalama Ohana Family History, 45.

22. *Deseret News,* July 16, 1862.

CONCLUSION

Through the course of these pages, you have met twelve remarkable women who contributed to the world in a myriad of ways. The light of these pioneers continue in us, the inheritors of their frontiers.

As I look at the world my daughter is growing into, there is no question women have come a long way. Each of these twelve women reacted differently to the constraints of their time. Some, like Charley and Luzena, played within the system and succeeded by its own rules. Others fought the status quo directly, like Abigail, Mother Jones, and Zitkala-Sa, demanding change. Still others, like Clara and Mary, simply lived lives that defied all expectations. Their examples illustrate that unfair systems need pressure from without and within in order to change.

A life viewed in retrospect, whether fictional or drawn from reality, tends to feel inevitable, as if it could not have happened any other way. But this inevitability is only an illusion of hindsight. The reality is that any of these stories could have had drastically different endings at any point of their narratives. Authors make constant choices in narration, just as each of us do day to day. Though many of our choices are influenced and constrained by culture, time, and place, I believe we have far more power to transcend these constraints than we realize. Cultivating bravery to defy expectations and live outside the status quo gives unspoken permission for others to do the same.

Exploring the lives of these women has been a profound privilege, one that leaves me marveling at the relevance of history to the world's contemporary struggles. Their "fugitive moments of compassion" have laid a foundation for us all to build on, reminding me that we are often our own best hero and worst enemy—as evil and goodness, hope and failure, coexist within each of our souls.

Here is an invitation to consider what type of story you are writing—and what the next chapter will be. From their examples, gather courage to use your talents and voice to build upon their efforts. The last chapter in this book is the one that will be written when you close these pages, for the story still unfolding is, of course, your own.

ACKNOWLEDGMENTS

When woman's true history shall have been written, her part
in the upbuilding of this nation will astound the world.
—Abigail Scott Duniway, *Path Breaking,* 1914,
Oregon Trail Museum, August 2015.

Every book that enters this world is an intense collaboration between many minds and talents. I am indebted to the librarians and historical societies that provided exhaustive resources for this book, including the library at BYU–Hawaii, the Washington County and Multnomah County libraries in Oregon, the LDS Church history library in Salt Lake City, the Oregon Historical Society, and the staff at the Donaldina Cameron House in San Francisco. I cannot say enough in praise of libraries and librarians; they wage peace and equity on behalf of a suffering world.

Many friends and family members read and responded to early drafts, including Marilynn A. Monson, Abigayle M. Ellison, Rachel Hall, Cheri Woods-Edwin, Brian King, and Jordan Rudd.

I was privileged to work with a talented team of editors and designers at Shadow Mountain, and I thank them for their efforts, particularly Lisa Mangum and Heidi Taylor, whose unfailing support and encouragement is every writer's dream.

I thank my children Nathan and Aria who so often inspire and support my work.

Finally, I thank the pioneering women and men of previous generations who fought and sacrificed for all the rights I enjoy today, including the ability to vote, attend college, and chase after my dreams.